ATHANASIUS OF ALEXANDRIA

CASCADE COMPANIONS

The Christian theological tradition provides an embarrassment of riches: from Scripture to modern scholarship, we are blessed with a vast and complex theological inheritance. And yet this feast of traditional riches is too frequently inaccessible to the general reader.

The Cascade Companions series addresses the challenge by publishing books that combine academic rigor with broad appeal and readability. They aim to introduce nonspecialist readers to that vital storehouse of authors, documents, themes, histories, arguments, and movements that comprise this heritage with brief yet compelling volumes.

RECENT TITLES IN THIS SERIES:

Feminism and Christianity by Caryn D. Griswold
Angels, Worms, and Bogeys by Michelle A. Clifton-Soderstrom
Christianity and Politics by C. C. Pecknold
A Way to Scholasticism by Peter S. Dillard
Theological Theodicy by Daniel Castelo
The Letter to the Hebrews in Social-Scientific Perspective
    by David A. deSilva
Basil of Caesarea by Andrew Radde-Galwitz
A Guide to St. Symeon the New Theologian by Hannah Hunt
Reading John by Christopher W. Skinner
Forgiveness by Anthony Bash
Jacob Arminius by Rustin Brian
The Rule of Faith: A Guide by Everett Ferguson
Jeremiah: Prophet Like Moses by Jack Lundbom
Richard Hooker: A Companion to His Life and Work by W. Bradford Littlejohn
Scripture's Knowing: A Companion to Biblical Epistemology by Dru Johnson
John Calvin by Donald McKim
Rudolf Bultmann: A Companion to His Theology by David Congdon
The U.S. Immigration Crisis: Toward an Ethics of Place
    by Miguel A. De La Torre
Theologia Crucis: A Companion to the Theology of the Cross
    by Robert Cady Saler
Theology and Science Fiction by James F. McGrath
Virtue: An Introduction to Theory and Practice by Olli-Pekka Vainio
Approaching Job by Andrew Zack Lewis
Reading Kierkegaard I: Fear and Trembling by Paul Martens
Deuteronomy: Law and Covenant by Jack R. Lundbom
The Becoming of God: Process Theology, Philosophy, and Multireligious Engagement by Roland Faber

ATHANASIUS OF ALEXANDRIA

An Introduction to his Writings and Theology

LOIS M. FARAG

CASCADE *Books* · Eugene, Oregon

ATHANASIUS OF ALEXANDRIA
An Introduction to his Writings and Theology

Cascade Companions

Copyright © 2020 Lois M. Farag. All rights reserved. Except for brief quotations in critical publications or reviews, no part of this book may be reproduced in any manner without prior written permission from the publisher. Write: Permissions, Wipf and Stock Publishers, 199 W. 8th Ave., Suite 3, Eugene, OR 97401.

Cascade Books
An Imprint of Wipf and Stock Publishers
199 W. 8th Ave., Suite 3
Eugene, OR 97401

www.wipfandstock.com

PAPERBACK ISBN: 978-1-4982-8256-7
HARDCOVER ISBN: 978-1-4982-8258-1
EBOOK ISBN: 978-1-4982-8257-4

Cataloguing-in-Publication data:

Names: Farag, Lois M., author

Title: Athanasius of Alexandria : an introduction to his writings and theology / Lois M. Farag.

Description: Eugene, OR: Cascade Books, 2020 | Series: Cascade Companions | Includes bibliographical references and index.

Identifiers: ISBN 978-1-4982-8256-7 (paperback) | ISBN 978-1-4982-8258-1 (hardcover) | ISBN 978-1-4982-8257-4 (ebook)

Subjects: LCSH: Athanasius, Saint, Patriarch of Alexandria, –373.

Classification: BR65.A446 F37 2020 (paperback) | BR65.A446 (ebook)

Manufactured in the U.S.A.   04/24/20

*To Athanasius of Alexandria
The theologian and spiritual mentor*

In praising Athanasius, I shall be praising virtue.
To speak of him and to praise virtue are identical...
In praising virtue, I shall be praising God,
Who gives virtue to men and lifts them up...

GREGORY NAZIANZUS, *ORATIONS 21*

CONTENTS

Abbreviations • ix
Introduction • xi

1 Athanasius of Alexandria: A Personal and Literary Biography • 1
2 The Incarnation, Creation, and Renewal • 25
3 Scripture • 53
4 The Trinity • 77
5 *Energeia* and *Theopoiēsis*: Activity and Making Divine • 111
6 The Spiritual Life, a Life of Renewal • 136

APPENDIX 1
Map of Roman Empire around the Mediterranean with cities mentioned in the life of Athanasius • 155

APPENDIX 2
The Creed • 157

Bibliography • 161
Subject Index • 165

ABBREVIATIONS

Apol. Const.	*Defense before Constantius (Apologia ad Constantium)*
Apol. Sec.	*Defense against the Arians (Apologia secunda, Apologia contra Arianos)*
C. Ar.	*Orations against the Arians (Orationes contra Arianos)*
C. Gent.	*Against the Pagans (Contra gentes)*
Decr.	*Defense of the Nicene Definition (De decretis)*
Dion.	*On the Opinion of Dionysius (De sententia Dionysii)*
Ep. Aeg. Lib.	*Letter to the Bishops of Egypt and Libya (Epistula ad episcopos Aegypti et Libyae)*
Ep. Adelph.	*Letter to Adelphius (Epistula ad Adelphium)*
Ep. Afr.	*Letter to the Bishops of Africa (Epistula ad Afros episcopos)*
Ep. encycl.	*Circular Letter (Epistula encyclica)*
Ep. Epict.	*Letter to Epictetus (Epistula ad Epictetum)*

Abbreviations

Ep. fest.	*Festal Letters* (*Epistula festales*)
Ep. Marcell.	Letter to Marcellinus on the Interpretation of the Psalms (*Epistula ad Marcellinum de interpretatione Psalmorum*)
Ep. Max.	*Letter to Maximus* (*Epistula ad Maximum*)
Ep. mon. 1 & 2	*First* or *Second Letter to the Monks* (*Epistula ad monachos*)
Ep. Serap.	*Letters to Serapion concerning the Holy Spirit* (*Epistula ad Serapionem*)
Fug.	*Defense of His Flight* (*Apologia de fuga sua*)
Inc.	*On the Incarnation* (*De incarnatione*)
Metaph.	Aristotle, *Metaphysics*
H. Ar.	*History of the Arians* (*Historia Arianorum*)
Hen. Som.	*Encyclical Letter of Alexander concerning the Deposition of Arius* (*Henos somatos*)
Hist.	Rufinus, *Eusebii Historia ecclessiastica a Rufino translate et continuata*
Hist. eccl.	Eusebius, *Historia ecclesiastica*, the same for Socrates and Sozomen, *Historia ecclesiastica*
LXX	Septuagint (the Greek translation of Scripture)
Princ.	Origen, *De principiis* (*Peri archon*)
Resp.	Plato, *Republic* (*Respublica*)
Syn.	*De synodis* (*On the Councils of Ariminum and Seleucia*)
Tom.	*Tomus ad Antiochenos* (*Tome to the People of Antioch*)
Vit. Ant.	*Life of Antony* (*Vita Antonii*)

INTRODUCTION

ATHANASIUS OF ALEXANDRIA IS a major figure in the history of Christian theology. He has been given titles such as "The Champion of Orthodoxy" for his contribution to the articulation of the Christian faith at a time of theological debate that rocked the universal church in the fourth century. Though his contribution to the understanding of the Trinity is foundational to Christian theology and his name is famous among early theologians, the details of his Trinitarian theology and the content of his writings are often unknown today and few of his books are on the bookshelves of systematic theologians, pastors, or inquiring Christian readers. C. S. Lewis correctly diagnosed the problem: "There is a strange idea abroad that in every subject the ancient books should be read only by the professionals, and that the amateur should content himself with the modern books . . . . This mistaken preference for the modern books and this shyness of the old ones is nowhere more rampant

Introduction

than in theology."[1] In his attempt to overcome the historical barrier, he wrote the introduction to a translation of *On the Incarnation* by Athanasius to help disseminate the text among a wider general audience. *On the Incarnation* is the most read of Athanasius's writings, followed by the *Life of Antony*. The rest of Athanasius's writings are still read by very few, mostly academics. Scholars of early Christianity have produced excellent research on Athanasius but their academically sophisticated work requires a person already well acquainted with the writings of Athanasius to appreciate their contribution to the subject matter. This book is an attempt to introduce Athanasius to a larger audience to generate interest and encourage readers to delve into the writings of this great thinker and theologian.

The Cascade Companions series, of which this book is a part, seeks to narrow the gap between the academy and broader ecumenical audiences. The term "introduction" in the subtitle points to the objective of this book. It is a guided introduction to the writings of Athanasius and not about what is written about Athanasius or those who have studied and written about Athanasius. The book incorporates the results of academic research by scholars who have spent time to understand the depth of Athanasius's writings and made valuable contributions, but to keep to the introductory nature and objectives of the series it has minimal citations and is concisely written.

The aim of this book is to introduce Athanasius's writings in an abridged and simplified form to help the reader navigate the labyrinthine, repetitive, and long-winded writing style characteristic of early Christian writers, who followed rhetorical rules different from our own. The reader is surprised when the author deviates into various subjects that might seem disconnected from the main topic. Such a

1. Athanasius, *On the Incarnation*, 3.

writing style is not conducive to the modern reader, who can easily lose track of the author's train of thought. The introduction aims to highlight the major historical, theological, biblical, and spiritual themes in Athanasius's writings so that the reader will be attentive to them when she encounters them. Properly understood, reading Athanasius is always rewarding.

In this book we focus on the main points that interested Athanasius and introduce ideas that became influential in later theological Christian thought, either historically or in modern times. The first four chapters introduce, as systematically as possible, some, not all, of the main points that shaped the writings of Athanasius. The book begins by introducing Athanasius through his writings and putting his writings into context. As most of his writings were written in response to heresies, accusations, or current events, the first chapter introduces the writings within the context of Athanasius's life story. We will see that Athanasius travelled to attend councils and meetings with the emperor, received letters from bishops throughout the empire, and was exiled for many years both within Egypt and outside it. A map in the appendix is marked with the cities and regions relevant to the life of Athanasius, giving the readers at a glance a sense of the huge distances Athanasius travelled. It also gives an idea of the extensive level of communications among bishops of the Roman Empire and the extent of the fame and influence Athanasius had among them. The map also conveys the spread of the Arian heresy across a vast geographical area and the extent to which it consumed the universal church.

Chapter 2 presents the main theological framework that guided all of Athanasius's writings: his vision of salvation and how the Word/Logos restored and renewed the image of God in humanity. This is the core message of

Introduction

Athanasius and a theme that recurs throughout the book. This vision provides the context within which the theology of Athanasius and his spirituality is to be understood. Chapter 3 is about the role of Scripture in Athanasius's theology; a topic that deserves more scholarly attention. The methods of interpretation explained in chapter 3 prepare the reader for the theological method Athanasius applied in his theology and help the reader navigate Athanasius's writing style and sequence of thought, which is primarily dependent on biblical texts.

Chapter 4 is about the Trinity. The Arian controversy was focused on the status of the Son and his equality to the Father. For Athanasius, the Arian proposition, though focused on the Son, affected the understanding of the Trinity and the whole of salvation. Athanasius works within a clear Trinitarian framework. He wrote one of the earliest expositions on the Holy Spirit. The theological terms that Athanasius uses and the main themes that concern him are well represented in the Nicene Creed, thus it was deemed helpful to include the creed in an appendix for the reader to read it in tandem with the chapter. The creed also highlights the tremendous impact of Athanasius's theology on the universal church.

The last two chapters are about themes of historical significance and of interest to modern scholarship and readers. Chapter 5 looks at Athanasius's understanding of *energeia* and *theopoiēsis*. These two concepts contributed to the understanding of the Trinity and its essence. For Athanasius *energeia* or activity is not limited to divine activity but is also relevant to the incarnation and the person of Christ. The aim of this chapter is not to discuss the later theological and historical significance of this term in Latin and Byzantine theology, which is beyond the scope of this introductory book, but rather to present Athanasius's contribution to the concept of *energeia*. Many claim that the term *theosis*, which has come to be of great interest to contemporary theologians in both east and west, is rooted in Athanasius's dictum, "he became human that we might be made god (*theopoiēthōmen*)." This chapter investigates how the term *theopoiēsis*, "making Divine," is expressed in Athanasius's own words. The reader interested in *theosis* will discern Athanasius's contribution and his distinctive thought on the topic. Thus, chapter 5 will be of interest to those interested in a more in-depth study of Athanasius and his impact on later theology.

The last chapter articulates, very briefly, the theological foundation of Athanasius's spirituality. It is based on his theological vision discussed in chapter 2. This chapter also highlights the interconnectedness of theology and spirituality; early Christianity did not compartmentalize religious ideas but viewed the person with a holistic vision in which theology, morality, spirituality, and biblical interpretation cannot be separated. Though here the topics are treated in separate chapters, the chapters feed off each other. Foundational theological themes have to be reiterated to highlight their connectedness in Athanasian thought. This chapter also discusses the relationship between personal and corporate spirituality within his writings.

Each chapter in the book presents more an outline of the subject matter than an in-depth study. Volumes have been written on each topic and the "Bibliographical Works" will be a great resource for the reader who wants to delve more deeply into Athanasian studies. At the end of each chapter, as well, there is a list of "Suggested Readings" designed to introduce the reader gradually to the long list of Athanasius's work. The accompanying readings do not suggest that other works are not important, but rather serve as a navigational tool. All of Athanasius's writings are rewarding to read.

I would like to thank Cascade editors for inviting me to contribute to the Cascade Companions series. The introduction of the treasures of Christian thought in an accessible, brief format is a project worthy of commendation.

1

ATHANASIUS OF ALEXANDRIA

A Personal and Literary Biography[1]

OUR KNOWLEDGE OF THE life of Athanasius is sparse and has many lacunae. On the other hand, his writings shed some light on aspects of the theological controversies of the fourth century and these writings would be better understood within the context of Athanasius's life. This chapter will weave the personal biography of Athanasius with his

1. The map in Appendix 1 shows cities Athanasius visited, cities whose bishops he corresponded with, cities to which he was exiled, locations of major synods and councils, and places relevant to imperial activity. The map demonstrates the scope of the interconnectivity and networks of early church leaders and the impact of Athanasius and his writings across the huge expanses of the Roman Empire as well as on the history of Christianity during the fourth century and later.

writings. In so doing, I hope to show the way his life provides context for the texts as well as how the texts shed light on his activity. Together the texts and contexts help explain the decisions he made and why his life unfolded in the way it did.

ATHANASIUS'S EARLY YEARS

Athanasius was born in Egypt around AD 295–98.[2] The end of the third and beginning of the fourth century was a critical and formative time in the history of Christianity. By the beginning of AD 303 severe persecution had erupted following a decree from the Roman Emperor Diocletian to destroy the churches, burn scriptures, imprison Christian leaders, and coerce Christians to offer sacrifice. Those who refused were tortured and others killed.[3] Pope Peter of Alexandria (300–311) was martyred during this persecution.[4] Alexandrian tradition considers Peter the "Seal of the Martyrs" and his martyrdom marks the end of persecution in Egypt. Martyrdom will have an impact on Athanasian theology as the faith of the martyrs demonstrates the power of the resurrection and the overcoming of death.[5] Soon after Peter's martyrdom, Emperor Constantine (r. 306–37) issued an edict of toleration of Christianity, known as the Edict of Milan (313), and churches began to experience peace.

---

2. Gwynn offers a summary of the scholarly arguments surrounding the chronology of Athanasius's life and writings. I will primarily follow the dateline of Gwynn, *Eusebians*, 13–48; and Gwynn, *Athanasius*, 1–17; while consulting Anatolios, *Athanasius*, 1–39; and Donker, *Apostolos*, 7–27.

3. Eusebius, *Hist. eccl.* 8:2, 3, 7, 8.

4. See Vivian, *Saint Peter of Alexandria*.

5. See chapter 2.

Athanasius of Alexandria: A Personal and Literary Biography

During the annual celebration commemorating the martyrdom of Peter of Alexandria, headed at the time by Pope Alexander of Alexandria (312–28), Athanasius and some of his friends were playing on the shore. They were reenacting baptism, with Athanasius playing a bishop baptizing some catechumens. Alexander observed Athanasius's careful reenactment of the ritual and called the young Athanasius to his presence. Alexander saw promise in the young Athanasius and oversaw his education in grammar and rhetoric.[6] A few scholars consider this story legendary, but its circulation shows that Athanasius was viewed at an early time as a person destined to lead the church during a critical period. Gregory Nazianzus mentions that Athanasius received a brief education of literature and philosophy. We do not have much information about the type of education Athanasius received, nor the depth of Greek philosophy and rhetoric he acquired. His writing style indicates he was very well versed in Scripture.[7] Alexander appointed Athanasius a deacon, then his secretary. Athanasius later accompanied him to the Council at Nicaea.[8] *The History of the Patriarchs* describes Athanasius as Alexander's "scribe," "interpreter," and "minster of the word."[9] During this pe-

---

6. Rufinus, *Hist.* 1.14; Socrates, *Hist. eccl.* 1.15, who mentions the story based on Rufinus' account; Sozomen, *Hist. eccl.* 2.17. Another legend describes Athanasius as a son of a rich non-Christian widow. She makes every attempt to marry him off, but he refuses. She discovers his devotion to Christianity and realizes that if she opposes him she will lose him. She eventually goes to Alexander and he baptizes her and her son Athanasius. *History of the Patriarchs of Alexandria, Patrologia Orientalis* 1:407–8. It should be noted that there is no evidence that he was a convert.

7. Gregory Nazianzus, *Orations* 21.

8. Socrates, *Hist. eccl.* 1.15.

9. *History of the Patriarchs of Alexandria, Patrologia Orientalis* 1:408.

riod when Athanasius was under the tutelage of Alexander, a presbyter by the name of Arius began to appear on the stage of history.

Arius was a presbyter in the city of Alexandria under the jurisdiction of Alexander. His preaching and his writings caused a lot of upheaval in Alexandria. Arius did not accept the full divinity of the Son, considering him a created being. His famous dicta, there was "once he (the Son) was not" and "he was not before his origination," summarize his theology. Our knowledge of Arius's ideas is through the remaining fragments of the *Thalia*[10] and a letter from Arius to Alexander, in addition to the rebuttal of his ideas throughout Athanasius's writings.[11] Alexander recognized the threat of such teachings on the understanding of the Trinity and salvation and convened a council in Alexandria (c. 321). The *Encyclical Letter of Alexander concerning the Deposition of Arius* mentions that all the bishops of Egypt and Libya, who were around a hundred in number, anathematized both Arius and his followers.[12]

Arius presented his case to other bishops in the Eastern Empire. Some bishops began taking sides with Arius and others with Alexander. Emperor Constantine decided to resolve the matter by calling all the bishops, within and outside the Empire, to a council at Nicaea in 325. It was the first time that bishops of all the churches met face to

10. *C. Ar.* 1:5–6; *Syn.* 15. Athanasius informs us that Arius wrote a *Thalia* to express his ideas and to encourage the Eusebians. Williams, *Arius*, 62–66, 98–116. Stead, "*Thalia* of Arius," 20–52.

11. *Syn.* 16. See chapter 4 for Arius's ideas. There are other writings from the followers of Arius's or the Eusebians that express the development of this theology but this is beyond the scope of this study.

12. *Hen. Som.* 3. The end of the letter expresses grief "for their destruction" but declares the necessity of such action based on Luke 21:8 and 1 Tim 4:1. *Hen. Som.* 5.

face. The wounds of the bishops who suffered torture during the period of persecution were visible to all who were present, giving more weight to their voice at the council. This council set a precedent for the emperor and the state to interfere in the affairs of the church. The emperor not only presided over the council, he also enforced its decrees. The council agreed on a "creed," the exile of Arius, and other matters concerning church organization. The Nicene Creed represented the orthodox faith of the church and those who accepted it returned to their episcopal sees; those who refused to sign it were exiled through imperial force. For the first time in the history of Christianity an emperor decided which bishop remained in his episcopal see and, even more, which faith was accepted in the empire. This policy would lead to the five exiles of Athanasius.

ATHANASIUS POPE OF ALEXANDRIA (328–73)

Alexander died in 328 and Athanasius, who was nominated by Alexander, became his successor. His ordination was contested by many who coveted the position of bishop of Alexandria. Alexandria was a major cultural and economic center in the empire and after the Council of Nicaea its theological leadership was unchallenged. The first theological school in the history of Christianity was in Alexandria. The Council of Nicaea affirmed the geographical extent of the Alexandrian Church as Egypt, Libya, and Pentapolis; in present day terms, Egypt and Libya.[13] There were about ninety bishops under the jurisdiction of Athanasius.[14] Alexandria was a cosmopolitan city, a main port and commercial center on the Mediterranean, and a major cultural

13. Canon 6 of the Council of Nicaea, and the Letter of the Synod of Nicaea to the Egyptians.

14. *Ep. Afr.* 10.

center for the whole Roman Empire. It was a philosophical center that hosted most of the philosophical schools of the time. It was a science center where the study of mathematics, astronomy, medicine, and the arts was unsurpassed in the empire. Because of the scientific skill of the Alexandrians, it was the yearly obligation of the pope of Alexandria to calculate and communicate to the churches the date to celebrate Easter. The *Festal Letters* of Athanasius attest to that practice. Egypt was also the breadbasket of the empire. Having the power to control the main sustenance of the empire played a role when Athanasius was later accused of threatening to stop the wheat shipment to Constantinople, a threat that the emperor did not take lightly, which caused a rift between the emperor and the bishop. These powers made many covet the position of pope of Alexandria. The Melitians, a schismatic group, exerted great efforts to wrest control of the Alexandrian episcopate.

Melitius of Lycopolis was of the opinion that those who lapsed during the Diocletian persecution should receive harsh punishment. Peter of Alexandria, on the other hand, argued for leniency. Though it was not a theological disagreement, it eventually led to a division in the Egyptian church. Melitius ordained presbyters beyond his diocesan jurisdiction who aligned with his position, which led Peter of Alexandria to excommunicate him. This division persisted until the Council of Nicaea when the council decreed through the *Synodical Letter to the Egyptians* that those bishops ordained by Melitius did not have authority to ordain any more presbyters without the consent of Pope Alexander. Those presbyters already ordained by Melitian bishops were to be examined and, if they had been chosen by the people and Alexander confirmed their election, they would keep their position. The Council's decree gradually resolved the Melitian problem but tension was still present at the time of the election of Athanasius as pope of Alexandria. Though the Melitians were weakened by the decree, they would contest the ordination of Athanasius. A remnant led by John of Acraph forged an alliance with Arian groups, leading to Athanasius's first exile.

We do not have much information about the early episcopal years of Athanasius. It is suggested that it was during this early period of his episcopal career that he wrote the two-part treatise *Against the Gentiles* and *On the Incarnation*. The treatise does not betray Arian concerns and thus some think it was written in 328 or earlier. The general scholarly consensus, however, now promotes the period of 328–333.[15] This two-part treatise presents the overarching theological vision of Athanasius and the theological foundation upon which the rest of his polemical writings should be understood.[16] Athanasius wrote his first *Festal Letter* in 329.

By the early 330s, the Melitians charged Athanasius with breaking a chalice, overturning a Melitian altar, and murdering a bishop by the name of Arsenius; they also charged that he was ordained to the bishopric below the canonical age of thirty. The latter charge has caused uncertainty among scholars about the date of Athanasius's birth. Constantine summoned Athanasius to court where he produced the allegedly murdered Arsenius, who had been hiding in Tyre. Constantine dismissed the charges against Athanasius.[17] By 334, Athanasius was accused with further charges. The new leader of the Arian bishops, Eusebius of Nicomedia, united with the Melitians against Athanasius

---

15. For the history of the debate, refer to Ernest, *Bible*, 423–24; and Leemans, "Athanasius Research," 132–35.

16. Because of the importance of this two-part treatise, chapter 2 is devoted to its theology.

17. *Festal Letter*, 4.5.

to form one front before Constantine. They persuaded Constantine that Athanasius would withhold the grain shipment from Alexandria to Constantinople. Constantine, alarmed by such a threat, called a synod at Tyre in 335 and exiled Athanasius to Trier in Gaul.[18] The synod restored the Melitians to church communion and accepted the Arian theology.

The imperial policies that began with the Council of Nicaea mark a new phase in the history of Christianity: Councils were called upon imperial demand and decisions were not based on theological orthodoxy. The emperor/state decided which bishops were convenient to the state and which were not and should be exiled. Churches became hostage to the state. In general, this was the case in the eastern part of the empire until its disappearance in the fifteenth century. In the west, the church was the only institution available to take over and fill the political vacuum after the fall of the western empire in AD 476. State interference in the eastern and western churches would diverge dramatically towards the end of the fifth century. The life of Athanasius was a manifestation of the new relationship between church and state.

ATHANASIUS'S FIRST EXILE (335–337)

Athanasius was exiled to Trier in 335 and remained there until the death of Constantine in 337. Arius died in 336.[19]

---

18. *Apol. Sec.* 87. This treatise was misnamed "*Apologia Secunda*" due to its placement after the *Apologia Fuga*. Gwynn, *Eusebians*, 16.

19. Athanasius wrote a *Letter to Serapion on the Death of Arius* around 339–346. The letter's main concern is that Arius did not die in communion with the church. It also mentions the famous story of Arius dying in Constantinople while fulfilling the "necessities of nature." The account of the death of Arius in a latrine is also mentioned in *Letters to the Bishops of Egypt and Libya* (*Epistula ad episcopos*

After Constantine's death, the empire was divided among his three sons: Constantinus (337–40), Constans (337–50), and Constantius (337–61). Constantinus, the western emperor, resided in Trier during the time of Athanasius's exile and got to meet Athanasius. On Athanasius's return from the first exile he met with Constantius, the emperor of the eastern empire. Our knowledge of Athanasius's first two exiles (335–37 and 339–46) comes primarily from his *Apologia contra Arianos*. The first part of the *Apologia* covers the period 338–47, and the second part, the period 328–37; the last few sections (89–90) cover the persecution and lapse of Liberius of Rome and Hosius of Cordova around 358. The structure of the text suggests that the first half was written around 347–51 and the second half around 338–40.[20] The *Apologia* is historical in nature and is a collection of documents assembled by Athanasius to prove his innocence against the Eusebian charges. The narrative that Athanasius provides in *Apologia contra Arianos* is the foundation for the ecclesial understanding of this period in both east and west.

Athanasius returned to Alexandria. He now called his opponents "Eusebians" as they were now led by Eusebius of Nicomedia. The Eusebians filed new accusations against Athanasius, claiming that he appropriated the returns from the wheat sale for his own funds. In 338 Athanasius traveled to Caesarea in Cappadocia to defend himself personally before emperor Constantius. Pope Julius of Rome supported Athanasius against the appointment of a new Arian bishop, by the name of Pistus, in Alexandria. Athanasius called for a council in Egypt (338) that issued a denunciation of the

---

Aegypti et Libyae).

20. Gwynn, *Eusebians*, 16–19.

appointment of Bishop Pistus and refuted all charges of financial wrongdoing against Athanasius.[21]

A new council convened in Antioch (339) during the time of the presence of emperor Constantius in Antioch in between his military campaigns in Mesopotamia. The council brought a new charge against Athanasius: that his return to Egypt was illegal as it was not ratified by a new ecclesial decision overturning the exile of the Council of Tyre. The council decided to replace Athanasius and sent the Arian Gregory of Cappadocia to Alexandria in his stead. Athanasius writes in the *Encyclical* that Philagrius, the Prefect of Egypt, suddenly issued a public letter, in the form of an edict, declaring that the court had ordered Gregory of Cappadocia to replace him. Athanasius describes such a proceeding as "novel" and "heard of for the first time." He blames the Eusebians for plotting his replacement and causing of his banishment.[22] Philagrius seized the churches and handed them over to Gregory. Crowds plundered the churches, a church and a baptistery were set on fire, monastics of both genders were subjected to physical violence, an altar was desecrated, and scriptures were burned.[23] Athanasius wrote this *Encyclical* in 339 before his departure to Rome, which began his second exile. In the *Encyclical* he warns the rest of the bishops that if the court takes such action against him and the Church of Alexandria there is nothing to stop the emperor from taking similar actions against the rest of the bishops. Athanasius warns other bishops that such action was new and threatened the church. He argues bishops should only be exiled for theological reasons based on charges from an ecclesial body not from a heretical group. He adds that any action

21. *Apol. Sec.* 3–20.
22. *Ep. encycl.* 2.
23. *Ep. encycl.* 3.

should be taken based on ecclesial canons and after inquiry in the presence of the laity and clergy who demanded the change.[24] Athanasius argues against the interference of the state in church affairs and warns other bishops of the repercussions of such policy. He pleads with them at the end of the *Encyclical* that if they let it pass unnoticed and do not take immediate action, this policy will extend to the rest of the churches, not only against Athanasius. This was a threat to the whole church.[25] Athanasius was right.

In his *History of the Arians* (c. 358), which covers events from 335–57, Athanasius continues the theme of the imperial imposition of bishops on churches. Athanasius describes the cruelty of Gregory, the imperially installed Arian bishop, towards the people in Alexandria and explains his behavior as based on his appointment by the court, accompanied by military power, rather than by apostolic tradition and according to ecclesiastical canons.[26] Athanasius tells us that the Council of Sardica issued a proclamation against Gregory of Cappadocia, who was sent by the emperor, saying that his ordination was not valid, the procedure of his appointment was novel and illegal in nature, and that his behavior did not make him even a Christian.[27] In his description of the attacks on himself and the imposition on Alexandria of Gregory and George by the court, Athanasius points out the hypocrisy of Constantius, who pretended to respect church canons but appointed bishops from court.

24. *Ep. encycl.* 2.
25. *Ep. encycl.* 6.
26. *H. Ar.* 13–14.
27. *H. Ar.* 17. Gregory Nazianzus would concur with Athanasius regarding the process by which bishops were chosen. Gregory wrote that people voted for bishops following the right of succession to the throne of Saint Mark, demonstrating how bishops were chosen in Alexandria. Gregory Nazianzus, *Orations* 21.8.

ATHANASIUS OF ALEXANDRIA

Athanasius opposed the imperial practice of imposing bishops who were neither voted for by the people nor from the people they would be serving; neither Gregory nor George were Egyptians. Athanasius asks: Where is the canon that gives the emperor the right to send soldiers to invade churches? What tradition allows courts and state appointees to exercise authority in ecclesial matters and, even worse, to falsify orders and make them bear the name of a bishop?[28] Athanasius's opposition to imperial rule over the church is demonstrated by the following questions: When did the church let the emperor validate its judgment? Or when were the decrees of the emperor recognized in the church? The fathers never sought imperial approval in any of the preceding synods nor did the emperor involve himself in church affairs.[29] Athanasius then attributes changes in imperial policies towards the church to heretics whom Emperor Constantius used to enforce his power over the church and who in turn used the emperor to enforce their power in the church.[30] In the second public protest, the people demand that the emperor order the prefect of Egypt to cease violence against the people and not to send any bishops except Athanasius, who was bishop according to the succession of the fathers of Alexandria.[31] Athanasius was fighting on two fronts: 1) the theological and 2) the political with regard to the relationship between church and state. All the questions Athanasius raised are very valid. It should be noted, however, that when Emperor Constantine called the first council, that of Nicaea, no bishop seemed to object to the interference of the empire. It is only when churches experienced the heavy-handedness of the state

28. *H. Ar.* 51.
29. *H. Ar.* 52.
30. *H. Ar.* 52.
31. *H. Ar.* 81.

and when decisions were not in their favor that Athanasius began to recognize the implications of such a policy. And he fought back.

ATHANASIUS'S SECOND EXILE (339–46)

The Council of Antioch exiles Athanasius to Rome. The second exile lasts about seven years (339–46) during which time Athanasius is in Rome, Milan, Trier, Sardica, Naissius, and Aquileia. Athanasius pens *Orations against the Arians* during his second exile. Though Arius had died in 336, his ideas did not die and were embraced in various forms by Eusebius of Nicomedia, Asterius the Sophist, and Marcellus of Ancyra, among others. In *Orations against the Arians*, Athanasius has in mind all the heresies that either stemmed from Arian thought or were lingering from previous controversies.[32] The first three orations are considered genuine while most scholars have agreed that the fourth cannot be attributed to Athanasius.[33] Athanasius begins the *Orations* with the presentation of the Arian thought as represented in the *Thalia*. He then defends the divinity of the Son, which is followed by an "orthodox" exegesis of a series of biblical passages that Arius misinterpreted. Proverbs 8:22 receives special attention, its exegesis taking up most of the second oration. The orations represent Athanasius's mature theological reflections.

In 341, Pope Julius convened a local synod in Rome that pronounced Gregory's appointment uncanonical. The synod also reinstated Marcellus of Ancyra after he wrote a confession of faith that was acceptable to the Roman synod.

32. See chapter 4.

33. For an overview of the dating of *Orations* see Leemans, "Athanasius Research," 138–44. For the authenticity of *Against the Arians* 3 see Ernest, *Bible*, 429–30.

Such moves from the west were not well received by the eastern bishops who considered that they overrode the decisions of the Council of Tyre, contravening the practice that the decisions of one council should not override the decisions of another. Pope Julius responded that, through the exile of Athanasius by the Council of Tyre, the bishops of the east had equally overridden the decisions of the Council of Nicaea. Pope Julius also presented another important defense of Athanasius. He argued that, since the church was at peace and all the bishops of Egypt were in unity with Athanasius, it was against apostolic tradition and church canons to send another bishop to replace Athanasius. In addition, the bishop that was sent was a stranger to the Egyptian church, had not been baptized in that church, was not known or voted for by the people or the clergy, and was sent from Antioch accompanied by soldiers and not by bishops of the church of Egypt. Even if Athanasius was guilty, the canons received from the Apostles should be followed and one of the clergy of the church of Egypt replace him, not an outsider.[34] This crucial development in state-church relations would affect the Church of Egypt for centuries to come and will be invoked later.

In the same year of 341, the eastern bishops gathered in Antioch to dedicate the golden-domed church built by Constantius. The eastern bishops took the opportunity to meet in what came to be called the "Council of Dedication" and issued three creeds in addition to a statement of faith by Theophronius of Tyana.[35] It should be observed that during the turmoil of the Arian controversy, between the Councils of Nicaea and Constantinople, when regional synods or councils met, they not infrequently issued creeds; more

---

34. *Apol. Sec.* 30.
35. *Syn.* 22–24.

than ten creeds were issued by various councils or synods. Only the Creed of Nicaea is considered orthodox.

In response, in 343 Emperor Constans of the west called for a council in Sardica. When the eastern bishop delegation arrived and found Athanasius attending the council, they demanded Athanasius withdraw from the council; the western bishops refused.[36] When Constantius defeated the Persians, the eastern bishops used it as an excuse to withdraw from the council to celebrate the victory with the emperor. On their way back, once they reached Philippopolis, within the eastern territories under the jurisdiction of Constantius, they excommunicated Athanasius of Alexandria, Marcellus of Ancyra, Julius of Rome, and Hosius of Cordoba. From Athanasius's *Letter 47* we can infer that each group of bishops claimed victory; the western bishops felt triumphant after the Council of Sardica, while the eastern bishops felt triumphant after the meeting in Philippopolis, as the eastern emperor sided with them. The confrontation between east and west had escalated and the bishops of east and west were exchanging excommunications rather than statements of faith and goodwill. There was a major division between Nicene and anti-Nicene churches.

Through the efforts of Constans, Constantius issued a letter to stop the persecution of the supporters of Athanasius in Egypt. The Arian bishop Gregory of Cappadocia died in 345 and Athanasius returned to his see in Alexandria. He entered Alexandria in triumph and was received

---

36. Athanasius sent two letters from Sardica to the Mareotis (*Letter 46*) and to the people of Alexandria (*Letter 47*). They give some account of the events in Sardica, especially the excommunication of Gregory, encourage and commend the people for keeping the Nicaean faith, and warn them against heretical teachings.

joyfully by his people and bishops. Athanasius remained in relative peace for the following decade.

A DECADE OF PEACE (346–56)

In this period of relative peace Athanasius had time to reflect on events and most probably also attend to the needs of the Church of Egypt after his long absence. Athanasius composed a few important writings during this period. We already noted that in the period of his first exile he started working on *Apologia contra Arianos*. He now completes this work. Athanasius starts working on the *History of the Arians* (*Historia Arianorum*), but will not be able to complete it until 357, that is during the first year of his third exile. The first four parts of the *History* cover the events 335–55 in chronological order. It covers the first and second exiles, the events at the synod of Sardica, the return of Athanasius to Alexandria, the death of Constans, and the Council of Milan. Parts five and six cover the lapse of both Liberius and Hosius of Cordoba, demonstrating the pressure exhibited on church leaders to recant the Nicene faith and accept Arianism. Part seven narrates the pressure and persecution that he himself endured leading up to his third exile. He ends the text with the persecutions the Egyptians endured for their Nicene faith and the arrival of George, the imperially appointed bishop to Alexandria after the exile of Athanasius.

Athanasius wrote *De decretis* (*Defense of the Nicene Definition*) between 350–56, that is, before his third exile and probably when Constantius was sole emperor. The text is in letter format addressed to a "learned man" who requested to know the events of the Council of Nicaea. By this time Athanasius had been exiled twice, many factions of Arianism had appeared, many regional synods were convened and had issued conflicting statements and put forth several creeds; the level of confusion among the laity and clergy must have been considerable. Athanasius had already written the *Orations against the Arians* followed by the *History of the Arians* to set the record straight. A further clarification concerning the Nicene Creed would be necessary at this point. Athanasius, in defense of the Nicene Creed, writes about the divinity of the Son, the titles used for the Son, and the necessity of using the non-scriptural term *homoousios* to stop the evasions of the Arians. Athanasius refers to earlier Christian writers like Origen of Alexandria and Pope Dionysius of Alexandria, thus affirming the use of tradition to defend his position. In continuation of the discussion in *De decretis*, Athanasius writes *De sententia Dionysii* in defense of his predecessor Dionysius of Alexandria who was not an Arian but did not use the term *homoousios*. The letter was most probably written around 354.

Athanasius wrote two letters towards the end of this period that show his pastoral side. In the *Letter to Dracontius*, he writes to Bishop Dracontius not to leave his flock. Athanasius explains that, after ordination, a bishop does not live for himself but for his flock and he is not to be a stumbling block to them. He also wrote the *Letter to Ammoun* in which he attempts to calm anxiety among the monks concerning nocturnal emissions, which were considered defiling.

Relations between Athanasius and Emperor Constantius were strained, though, as previously mentioned. They were eased briefly through the efforts of Emperor Constans. Emperor Constans, however, was murdered in 350 during a coup by Magnentius. Athanasius now lost his major political support. In 353, Constantius defeated Magnentius and became the sole ruler of the Roman Empire. In February

356 soldiers attacked the Church of Theonas while Athanasius was presiding over a service. Athanasius fled and hid in the Egyptian desert, thus beginning his third exile (356–62). Another stranger, George of Cappadocia, was installed as the Arian bishop in Alexandria. The people did not welcome him and he was chased out of the city in 358. At the news of the death of Emperor Constantius in 361, he was killed by rioters, both Christians and pagans.

Athanasius wrote two letters of defense: one to Emperor Constantius (*Defense before Constantius*) regarding the accusations against him, and the second defending the reason for his flight from Alexandria after the Church of Theonas attack (*Defense of His Flight*). His *Defense before Constantius* (*Apologia ad Constantium*) was written in several stages and refers to his previous writing, *Apologia Contra Arianos*. It affirms that all the accusations against him have proven invalid. Athanasius defends himself against the charges of slandering Emperor Constantius, denying correspondence with Magnentius, and praying in an undedicated church. Athanasius praises the emperor for inviting the injured party, Athanasius, to defend himself. At the end of the letter he defends his flight from Alexandria in 356, a theme that he will continue in his *Defense of His Flight* (*Apologia de fuga sua*). In the latter, Athanasius lists the atrocities of the Arians against the Nicene people and clergy of Alexandria. He then defends his flight by Scriptural references starting with Christ himself, who fled to Egypt and then from his persecutors until it was time for his crucifixion. He also gives other scriptural examples of prophets and finally the example of Christian martyrs. Athanasius argues there is a time to flee and a time to stay. The *Festal Letters* of this period portray Athanasius solving a dispute about the calendar for the Easter celebration and ordaining bishops, whose names and appointment he distributes to the rest of the church. It is interesting to note that in *Festal Letter 27*, written in 355, after years of suffering for the Nicene faith and a year before his flight, he titles himself "Bishop of Alexandria and Confessor." He considered the title "confessor," indicating his suffering for the faith, equal in honor to that of "bishop."

ATHANASIUS'S THIRD EXILE (356–62)

The third exile was the most prolific period for Athanasius and was accompanied by theological developments in the Arian debate that became more complicated with political interference. The *Letter to the Bishops of Egypt and Libya* was written after his flight (356) and before the arrival of the Arian George of Cappadocia (357). As a reminder to the bishops, he gives an overview of the Arian heresy and the *Thalia*. Athanasius warns the bishops in his jurisdiction not to sign a newly circulating Arian creed and exhorts them not to give in under pressure. He argues that if the Arians produce a yearly creed, they are not sure of their beliefs; otherwise, why rewrite their faith at every meeting?[37] To emphasize the heretical nature of their theology he refers to the developing alliance between the two heterodox factions, the Arians and the Melitians, and describes the dishonorable death of Arius in a latrine. During this period he also completed his *Defense before Constantius* and the *Defense of His Flight*.

Athanasius wrote the following major works during his third exile: as previously mentioned, *History of the Arians* (*Historia Arianorum*), begun during the decade of peace, was completed in 357; *On the Councils of Ariminum and Seleucia* (*De synodis*); *Letters to Serapion concerning the Holy Spirit* (*Epistula ad Serapionem*); and *Life of Antony*

---

37. *Ep. Aeg. Lib.* 1.6.

(*Vita Antonii*). The latter is one of his most read books. It is also significant that it is a new genre of hagiographical writing and very distinct from the rest of Athanasius's literary output. The hagiography of Antony is not just the narrative of a life, but rather a theological and spiritual guide to the Christian life. Its spiritual impact and its influence on the understanding of monasticism, especially in Egypt, is significant to the present day.[38]

The letter *De synodis* was written during the Councils of Ariminum and Seleucia (359), in the year of what came to be called the "dated" creed. Sections 30 and 31 were inserted after the death of Constantius. The theological context within which these councils convened is rather complicated. Aetius and Eunomius promoted the notion that the Son is unlike (*anomios*) the Father, for the Son is Begotten (*gen(n)ētos*) while the Father in essence is unoriginate (*agen(n)ētos*). Consequently, the Holy Spirit is created. This "Anomian" position is in contrast to the "homoian" position that the Son is "like" (*homoios*) the Father.[39] Basil of Ancyra added further nuances to the theological discussion at the time, promoting the term *homoiousios* (like according to essence) based on his understanding of the likeness of the Son to the Father as based on likeness of essence. Constantius advocated the opinion of Basil of Ancyra over that of Aetius and Eunomius and exiled them. Constantius called a council with the eastern bishops meeting in Seleucia and the western bishops, in Ariminum. Before the councils convened on May 22, 359, a creed was

---

38. See chapters 2 and 7; see also Farag, *Balance*, 62–94.

39. Anatolios, *Athanasius*, 27–28. This was further complicated with the Nicene group suspecting the use of *agenētos*, meaning unoriginate, to be of pagan origin in contrast to *agennētos* meaning ungenerate/unbegotten. See G. W. H. Lampe, ed. *A Patristic Greek Lexicon*, (Oxford: Clarendon Press, 1961) s.v. *agenētos* and *agennētos*.

written (thus called the "Dated" Creed), influenced by the theology of Basil of Ancyra and reflecting a compromise statement. The eastern bishops could not accept the compromise creed. The western bishops did not accept the necessity of a new creed and sent a delegation to that effect to Emperor Constantius who refused to meet with them for a long time. Constantius detained them first in Ariminum and then in Nice without giving them permission to return to their sees. The western bishops eventually relented and signed the document in Nice (the Creed of Nice) in order to return to their sees. At this point of history, both east and west signed the Arian Creed of Nice and thus the whole world became Arian except for Athanasius, who was in exile. Thus the famous lamentation of Jerome: "The whole world groaned, and was astonished to find itself Arian."[40]

The content of *De synodis* reflects the turmoil just described. In Part 1 Athanasius gives a detailed account of the double councils in Ariminum and Seleucia. Part 2 gives the history of the ten creeds issued by the Arians: the Dedication Creed, the Lucianic Creed, the Creed of Theophronius, the revision of the Nicene Creed in 342, the first and second Sirmium creeds, the Creed of Acacius in Seleucia, the Dated Creed, the Creed of Nice, and finally the Anomean Creed published under the patronage of Cosntantius in Antioch in 361. Part 3 appeals to the semi-Arians, like Basil of Ancyra, for reconciliation though insisting on the authority of the Nicene Creed. Further notes were added to the document after the death of Constantius in 361. *De synodis* is a significant document about the history of Arianism and the incessant theological debates that ripped the church apart during the fourth century.

An equally important document is the *Letters to Serapion concerning the Holy Spirit* (*Epistula ad Serapionem*)

---

40. Jerome, *Lucif.*, 19.

composed of three letters written 358–59. Athanasius defended the divinity of the Son and now defends that of the Holy Spirit, for whom not much credit is given. The Tropikoi denied the divinity of the Holy Spirit. For Athanasius, blasphemy against one person of the Trinity is blasphemy against the whole Trinity. To prove the divinity of the Holy Spirit Athanasius provides the correct exegesis of verses such as Amos 4:13 and 1 Timothy 5:21, which, he argues, the Tropikoi misinterpreted. The *Letters to Serapion* influenced the writings of Basil of Caesarea and Gregory Nazianzus, whose writings shaped the outcome of the Council of Constantinople in 381, which asserted the divinity of the Holy Spirit and added a passage to the Nicene Creed to affirm that. Gregory Nazianzus gives full credit to Athanasius when he writes: "he [Athanasius] was the first and only one, or with the concurrence of but a few, to venture to confess in writing, with entire clearness and distinctness, the Unity of the Godhead and Essence of the Three Persons, and thus to attain in later days, under the influence of inspiration, to the same faith in regard to the Holy Spirit, as had been bestowed at an earlier time on most of the Fathers in regard to the Son."[41]

Constantius died in 360 and his cousin Julian succeeded him. In February 362, Julian allowed all bishops to return to their sees, and Athanasius returned to Alexandria.

THE FINAL YEARS (362–73)

Athanasius's return to Alexandria was short as Emperor Julian forced Athanasius into exile in October 362. This marks his fourth exile. Julian died during battle with Persia in 363. When Jovian (363–64) took over the reign of the empire, Athanasius made a trip to Edessa to meet the emperor.

---

41. Gregory Nazianzus, *Orations* 21.33.

Letter 56 gives an account of the meeting with Emperor Jovian in which Athanasius emphasizes the Nicene faith and lists the provinces that accepted the faith of Nicaea ranging from as far north as Britain, as far west as Spain, to Asia and Cappadocia and all the provinces in between, including the Mediterranean. Athanasius returned to Alexandria after securing a document guaranteeing his position.

When Emperor Jovian died in 364, Valens took control of the Eastern Empire. Valens (364–78), an anti-Nicene, ordered all bishops who returned from exile during the time of Jovian to leave their sees. Athanasius did not acquiesce to the orders but Valens persisted. By the time the commander attacked the Church of Dionysius to arrest Athanasius, he had already left the church and his fifth and last exile began. Valens faced political unrest that threatened his position and in an attempt to control and calm the political turmoil, at least in Egypt, he gave permission for Athanasius to return to his see of Alexandria.

During this time Athanasius continued his literary output. Athanasius's focus on Scripture is one of the signatures of his writing method, and his *Festal Letter 39* (367) betrays such interest by listing the biblical books accepted in the church; the list of New Testament books corresponds to our present New Testament canon. In the *Letter to Adelphius* (c. 370), Athanasius defends the inseparability of the humanity and divinity of Christ; otherwise, we would be worshiping a creature and not the Son of God. The *Letter to Epictetus of Corinth* (c. 372) explains the impact of the full humanity of the person of Christ in the scheme of our salvation. These two letters are most influential as they will guide the theological debates of the fifth century. The writings of Athanasius are foundational for defining the theology of the Church of Alexandria throughout its history.

Athanasius dies in peace in 373. His authority and the orthodoxy of his theology is acclaimed at the end of his life and throughout history. Already during the time of Emperor Jovian, his renown, orthodoxy, and authority as a theologian is acknowledged by many. He is called the Champion of Orthodoxy, the Defender of Orthodoxy, and the Pillar of Faith. The Coptic Orthodox Church gives him the title "The Apostolic."

QUESTIONS FOR FURTHER DISCUSSION

- How did the events of the fourth century reveal Athanasius's character, theological acumen, and faith?
- The Arian controversy and political strife provided the context of Athanasius's writings. Explain how these historical events shaped the content of Athanasius's literary corpus.
- The Arian controversy and its aftermath definitely changed the relationship between church and state. Reflect on this change and compare and contrast East and West church/state dynamics.
- What was the process of electing the popes/bishops of the Church of Alexandria?

SUGGESTIONS FOR FURTHER READING

Defense against the Arians (*Apologia contra Arianos*)
History of the Arians (*Historia Arianorum*)
Defense of the Nicene Definition (*De decretis*)
On the Councils of Arminum and Seleucia (*De synodis*)
Letters 46, 47, 56
Festal Letters

2

THE INCARNATION, CREATION, AND RENEWAL

THE TWO-PART TREATISE *AGAINST the Gentiles* and *On the Incarnation*, together with the *Life of Antony*, are the most read texts of the Athanasian literary corpus and have had a large theological and spiritual impact throughout history. They represent a different literary genre than the rest of Athanasius's polemical writings. The surviving writings of Athanasius are mostly apologetic in defense of the faith against the Arian claims and addressed to those involved in the Arian debate such as secular leaders, ranging from emperors to local governors, bishops, and clergy. The two-part treatise, however, specifically addresses pagans, Jews, and Christians, the three categories encompassing the majority of the Roman Empire's population at that time. *The Life of Antony* addresses "brethren" living abroad, though this does not exclude those outside monastic communities from reading the *Life*.¹ Athanasius's style of writing is heavily influenced by the Bible, but since his intention in these treatises is to address a larger audience, his arguments follow patterns of contemporary logical thinking and generally accepted Platonic and other ancient Greek philosophical concepts.

Against the Gentiles discusses four main themes: the origin of evil, idolatry, the human soul endowed with reason, and God as creator of the universe. These themes lead to the discussion of the necessity of the incarnation in his second volume, *On the Incarnation*. In the latter, he gives a full theological vision of the unfolding of the incarnation, the crucifixion, and the resurrection. The resurrection overcame death, granted immortality, renewed God's image and likeness within humanity, and gave humanity the gift of renewal that has the power to change lives. This is how Athanasius expresses salvation. For Athanasius, who witnessed the severe persecution of Christians and how they gave their lives without fear of death, martyrdom was the greatest witness to the power of the resurrection, which overcame death, as death is not feared anymore and has no hold on humanity. When Athanasius speaks about the incarnation, crucifixion, and resurrection theologically, he is not engaged in a mental exercise but conveys a deep spiritual

1. Augustine, in his book *Confessions*, provides the most famous example of the influence of the *Life of Antony* on people beyond the monastic community and beyond the Christian faithful. Augustine writes that Ponticianus, who held high office in the court, introduced the story of Antony the Egyptian to Augustine and his friend Alypius. Augustine was amazed by Antony's way of life. When he began to read the *Life of Antony*, he was "set on fire," had a moment of conversion, and wanted to pursue an ascetic life (*Conf.* VIII.vi [14–15]). This narrative in Augustine's *Confessions* informs us that Antony's example deeply moved three lives to a life of holiness, Ponticianus, Alypius, and Augustine, and in the case of Augustine, even to conversion to Christianity.

experience that gives renewal and leads to a life of holiness. The *Life of Antony* gives a concrete living example of the power of renewal of the resurrection in the life of the Christian. Antony overcame all distractions, whether mental or physical, that would separate him from God. He renounced all his possessions, separated himself physically from worldly distractions, devoted his mind, soul, and heart to God, and reached a status of purity of life and soul through the power of renewal of the resurrection. He attained the status of humanity endowed with the image of God, before the transgression of the commandment. For the Son of God was made human so that we can be made divine.[2] This is the overarching theological framework of the two-part treatise of *Against the Gentiles* and *On the Incarnation* together with the *Life of Antony*. Even the polemical writings consumed with the Arian controversy should be understood within this larger theological framework. This chapter will unpack some of the main themes that contributed to this overarching theological vision of Athanasius.

THE SOUL AND THE ORIGIN OF EVIL

Athanasius did not write, nor did he attempt to write, a comprehensive understanding of the person, or a treatise on the soul. His interest in the soul emerges from his search for the origin of evil and how to understand the biblical concept of humanity as created in God's image and likeness. It will also be observed that there are Platonic and other Greek philosophical concepts underlying his understanding of the soul. These philosophical concepts, which shaped the mindset of the time, are considered normative and are taken for granted.

---

2. *Inc.* 54. This is Athanasius's most quoted dictum and encapsulates his understanding of the incarnation.

ATHANASIUS OF ALEXANDRIA

Athanasius begins the treatise of *Against the Gentiles* with the following:

> Evil does not exist from the beginning, nor even now is it found among the saints nor does it exist at all with them. But it was men who later began to conceive of it and imagine it in their own likeness.[3]

Athanasius strongly asserts that God is not the origin or creator of evil. Everything apart from the divine is a created entity. God is the creator, who created everything out of nothing,[4] thus everything that exists has its origin in God. If evil has a separate and independent existence, then God created evil or there is another cause of creation, that is, there is an independent, powerful evil god. Athanasius does not want to attribute to evil a real, physical existence. If evil exists, it has to come from God. God is all goodness and all

---

3. *C. Gent.* 2. Athanasius, *Contra Gentes and De incarnatione*, 5. Athanasius writes that the church's theology asserts that evil is neither from the beginning with God nor in God; nor has it any substantive existence. *C. Gent.* 7. The problem of evil has been addressed by a few of the early church writers, including Basil of Caesarea and Augustine of Hippo. In *Homily IX*, Basil demonstrates that God is not the creator of evil. He addresses the verses that mention God as the creator of evil and concludes that the origin of evil is in our free will. Augustine of Hippo was obsessed with the problem of evil. He was a Manichean before converting to Christianity and the Manicheans solved the problem of evil by suggesting that there are two opposing, equally powerful gods, the god of evil/darkness and the god of good/light. The Manichaean worldview was partly what Athanasius was confronting when he insisted that evil has no material presence. Augustine, after his conversion, had to find a Christian response to evil and formulated his theory on theodicy. He rejected the idea that evil can exist in itself and affirmed that evil came through humans choosing evil by their own free will (*Conf.* VII.v[7]–xv[21]). In Augustine's opinion departing from God takes away all goodness from humanity.

4. *Inc.* 3.

his creation is good. Evil does not come from good, nor is it in good.[5] God did not create evil, and if God because of his goodness did not create evil, then evil does not exist. Good is what is and evil is what is not. For the God who is, is what is good, and evil consists of the inner thoughts of humans.[6] This responds to the important question, What is the source of evil? Athanasius asserts that evil came to be when people conceived of it. This is where Athanasius turns to the study of the concept of the soul and the state of humanity at the beginning of creation.

Athanasius did not write a specific treatise about the soul, so we must glean his views on the soul from his other writings. He believes that the person is bipartite, composed of a body and a soul. His understanding of the "soul" is rather complex. Athanasius asserts that God is the creator of the soul.[7] He understands the death of the body as the separation of the soul from the body.[8] The soul, while not moved by other things, moves the body in a spontaneous movement, and this spontaneous movement continues even after separation from the body, i.e. after death. Since the movement of the soul is independent of the body, and moved by itself, then the soul outlives the body. The body dies when the soul departs from it.[9] The soul is immortal.[10]

5. *C. Gent.* 6.

6. *C. Gent.* 4, 7, 8.

7. *C. Gent.* 35. Athanasius differs from Plato who believed in the preexistence of the soul.

8. *C. Gent.* 3.

9. *C. Gent.* 33.

10. Socrates was the first to suggest the immortality of the soul. Plato mentions Socrates in the *Republic*, asking the astonished Glaucon: "Have you never perceived that our soul is immortal and never perishes?" *Resp.* 608d. In *Contra Gentes*, Athanasius displays a strong conviction that the soul is immortal. In *De incarnatione*, however, he explains the fall as death and non-existence (*Inc.* 4). If he speaks

The movement of the soul is its life, for when the body is in a very deep sleep the soul is in movement and is awake by virtue of its own power that transcends the nature of the body. The soul does not abandon the body when it transcends it to contemplate higher things and meets and converses with unembodied saints and angels through the purity of its mind. The immortal soul always contemplates things eternal and immortal. If this is the power of the soul while still attached to the body, how much more knowledge will it have about its immortality when freed from that body? Thoughts of immortality never abandon the soul. This is why the soul has the capacity to contemplate and behold God and receive from within itself the knowledge of the Word of God.[11]

God is within us, for the kingdom of God is within us.[12] Having the kingdom within us, the soul sees and perceives the King of the universe and "the saving Word of the Father."[13] The soul appears to be the seat of the intellect, the seat of rationality and reason. The soul endowed with intellect will recognize God as its maker and creator, and

---

about death, we should understand it as the separation of the soul from the body, but non-existence seems to indicate the death of the soul. With the incarnation, crucifixion, and resurrection human nature is renewed and humanity regains immortality. The immortality granted by the resurrection includes both soul and body, a privilege that the paradisiac humans did not have. This might explain why he sometimes speaks of the immortality of the soul while in other passages the emphasis is on immortality granted by redemption to both elements of human nature, body and soul. Athanasius maintains that the church teaches that the body is mortal while the soul is immortal. *C. Gent.* 33. Athanasius does not support this assertion by biblical references; he relies on the philosophical concepts that permeate the culture of his time.

11. *C. Gent.* 33.
12. Luke 17:21.
13. *C. Gent.* 30.

either acknowledges or denies God.[14] Athanasius asserts that each member of humankind has a soul and that the soul is rational.[15] The *nous* is the rational part of the soul that comprehends and has knowledge of God. The *nous*, which is connected to the soul, appears to reside within it.[16] From the Platonic view of the soul and Athanasius's clear bipartite understanding of the human person, we infer that Athanasius believes that the soul is the source of power, movement, and life within a person. The *nous* is immortal like the soul and informs the soul of God and what is right and wrong.[17]

Humans are rational animals, an indication that their soul is rational. Athanasius builds on this concept and asserts that because of reason, a person can reflect and comprehend things external to oneself. Humans judge and reflect on what they see and perceive by their bodily senses,

14. *C. Gent.* 26.

15. *C. Gent.* 30.

16. The Greek word *nous* has many connotations and more than one meaning can be implied within one usage. In the linguistic sense *nous* generally means *mind* as perceiving and thinking. It is also used to mean "to have sense" or "be sensible," or to have one's *mind* directed to something. It might also indicate the "heart." Also, it can mean "reason," "intellect," or 'thought." See Henry George Liddell, et al., eds. *A Greek-English Lexicon*, (Oxford: Clarendon, 1996) s.v. νόος.

17. Plato in the *Republic* introduces a soul that has three parts or aspects: reason, spirit, and appetite. These three parts could have conflicting motives. For example, a thirsty person has the appetite to drink but reason will oppose drinking because it is bad for the person. In this example, there are two opposing elements at work. The spirited element of the soul is like "sense of honor" or takes the side of reason against appetite, but it cannot be identified with reason. *Resp.* 434d-441c. In contrast, Athanasius speaks about two parts not three, but uses the concept of a multi-part soul familiar at that time. Similarly, Paul writes about the inner struggle caused by two conflicting aspects within him: "So I find it to be a law that when I want to do what is good, evil lies close at hand" (Rom 7:21). All biblical references are from the NRSV unless otherwise noted.

and then master their impulses by reason based on what seems best to them. While the senses can see, smell, touch, or taste, it is up to the soul, by the reason residing in it, to decide what to see, smell, touch, or taste. As a musician has many strings on his instrument and uses them intelligently to produce music, so the soul, when guided by an understanding mind, uses the senses to determine its actions. For example, the eye decides to turn its vision from one object to another.[18]

Athanasius furthers the discussion on the concept of the rational soul, or the soul endowed with reason/*nous*, in the discussion of spirituality and eternal life. While humans are aware of the mortality of the body, they contemplate immortality and virtue, things external and beyond the body.[19] When the body is at rest and quiet, the inward movement of the soul beholds what is outside itself.[20] Athanasius observes that the body is inwardly aware of higher things through the rational soul. Because of this, the body acts sometimes against its natural instincts because the rational soul guides it and directs it to other things or actions. The rational soul drives the body.[21]

In the beginning, God created humanity in his own image, through the Word, and gave humanity knowledge of God's eternity. When God created the universe and all that is in it out of nothing through his own Word, out of his goodness he gave special privilege to humans, a special grace, by making them in his image and likeness; that is, God gave them a share in the power of his own Word (*Logos*), thus making them rational (*logikoi*) beings. With this grace, rational humanity is able to perceive God and live

18. *C. Gent.* 31.
19. *C. Gent.* 32.
20. *C. Gent.* 31.
21. *C. Gent.* 32.

in blessedness and in fellowship with God and the saints. God had also endowed humanity with free will so humans could choose which way to go.²² For Athanasius, what is distinctive about humanity is that humans are made in God's image and likeness and are rational. This rationality, their power to choose, and their ability to comprehend God through the Word is what it means to be in God's image and likeness.

Humans have the power to choose between contemplation of God and indulging in the senses of the body. The knowledge of divine eternity and the constant contemplation on the divine makes it possible for humanity not to depart from God but to be in constant fellowship with the saints. When the soul is in a pure state, it constantly contemplates the image of the Father's word and lives a blessed and immortal life.²³ A person preserves a pure life when one transcends all things of the senses through the power of the mind. In this purity nothing hinders one's fellowship with God.²⁴ This was the state of the first Adam. But humans preferred to indulge in their bodily pleasures to contemplating God; consequently, they forgot the power they had from God. They turned away from God. When they turned away, they departed from God and fell into physical lust; this is when they knew they were naked and were ashamed. They were naked because they were stripped from contemplation on the divine. Humans, after discovering their nakedness, clung more to their desires. Desires made the soul weak and

---

22. *Inc.* 3.

23. There is resonance with such an idea in Origen, *Princ.* 1.1.9. who explains based on Matt 5:8 that to see God is to see him in the heart, and to understand God is to know him with the mind.

24. *C. Gent.* 2.

fearful of mortality. The weakened soul committed murder and other wrongful deeds.[25]

The weakened soul departs from the contemplation of the things of the intellect, what is perceptible to the mind, to the contemplation of pleasure, mistaking it for the good. The soul, whether in fellowship with God or not, does not lose its power of movement. When virtue does not guide the soul's movement, it rejects good and entertains evil. Good is what is while evil is what is not.[26] Athanasius assumes the preconceived philosophical idea that the divine is the unmovable mover. The unmovable divine reflects the divine's unchangeable essence. Thus, the creator does not move from good to evil while created beings are moved and move from good to evil or the other way.[27] Whether the soul is weak or guided by the *nous* towards goodness, its power of movement is part of its essence.[28] The soul, then, can choose to move away from desire, move away from all evil that affects it, and regain the purity it had at the time of its creation. The soul contemplates the word of the Father since it was created in the image of God and his likeness.[29]

Athanasius begins with the assertion that God, through the word, creates the human being from nothing and in a state of purity. Humans are composed of a body and a soul. The soul is endowed with reason/*nous* by which

25. *C. Gent.* 3.

26. *C. Gent.* 4.

27. For further reading on the concept of the "unmovable mover" refer to Aristotle's *Metaphysics* especially *Metaph.* 12. 6–9.

28. Athanasius writes that the soul moves the senses. It moves the eye to see, the ear to hear, and the hand to touch, and even the smell to receive odors. The soul moves the senses to act with other parts of the body like the feet to walk. *C. Gent.* 43. Athanasius also writes that just as the body grows the soul endowed with reason moves. For Athanasius, movement is part of the essence of the soul. *C. Gent.* 44.

29. *C. Gent.* 34.

it contemplates God. When the soul moves away from God it falls into its desires. This is the source of evil, as evil has no substantive existence, lest God the creator of all things should be the source of evil. Athanasius asserts that the soul through the *nous* within it can move towards the contemplation of God until it regains its purity. If the soul is unable to reach this level of purity through its own reasoning then further knowledge of God can be attained through Scripture or through creation. Creation can lead the soul to its creator. When humans failed to learn about God from creation, the incarnation of the Son of God became necessary, for the Word had to be incarnate to reveal the Father to humanity. In the following sections we will thus discuss the revelation of God through creation and the incarnation.

CREATION AS REVELATION OF GOD

Athanasius looks at creation, or the universe, through a theological lens. He speaks about creation in its relationship to God and humanity. Athanasius understands creation in its broadest sense as everything that God created. He writes that the invisible and incomprehensible God, who created all things and is beyond all that is created, wanted to reveal himself to humankind out of his lovingkindness toward them. God, by his own Word, gave order and harmony to the created universe so that his works reveal his invisible nature. God did not leave himself unknown, but revealed himself through the *nous* within the human soul and through the orderly nature of his creation. For who, Athanasius asks, can see the rising sun and the shining moon together with the stars moving within their orbits and not perceive the creator guiding them?[30] Who would not marvel at the successive seasons, which are contrary

---

30. *C. Gent.* 35.

to one another, for one season chills and the other burns, yet balance one another for the benefit of humankind and thus reveal the balancing work of the creator?[31] Athanasius gives various examples of things that might seem to be of opposite natures yet unite to reveal the harmonious nature of the universe that proclaims God to humanity: wet and dry, round and straight, fire and cold, earth and sea.[32] This harmony and consistency also indicate that there is one creator rather than many. Athanasius is defending the one God against the polytheistic, idol-worshipping society surrounding him.[33] If there is only one God, then other gods are not true gods. The true God is the Lord of Creation, who through his own Word established the harmony of creation.[34] Athanasius emphasizes that the Word/*Logos* he is referring to is not the seminal logos (*spermatikos logos*), the principle inherent in all creation that has no life or power of reason (*nous*).[35] Nor is he referring to the art of rhetoric that uses words/*logoi* as means of human expression. Athanasius is referring to the living and acting God (*zōnta kai energē theon*), the Word of the God of the universe.[36] Because of the multiple linguistic meanings of the word *logos* and the various ways that *logos* has been referred to in philosophical discourse, Athanasius intentionally distinguishes between the Stoic *spermatikos logos* or the *logos* used by rhetors and the Logos who is the Son of God, the Image of the Father, the creator of the universe, through whom all creation came to be.

31. *C. Gent.* 36.
32. *C. Gent.* 37.
33. *C. Gent.* 38, 39.
34. *C. Gent.* 40.
35. *Spermatikos logos* is a Stoic term referring to the generative principle of creation in Stoic thought.
36. *C. Gent.* 40.

The Incarnation, Creation, and Renewal

The Word exists in all things, his power is everywhere, he holds all creation in himself, he illuminates the visible and invisible, and he gives life to everything created.[37] God did not bring things into existence and then leave them on their own to perish by falling into non-existence. Rather, through the ordering of the Word, creation remains secure.[38] The Word, together with the Father, is unmoved but moves all things according to what seems good to the Father. Though things move in different directions, the Word moves all things at once, creating harmony in the world.[39] Athanasius gives the example of the movement of planets and stars: while they appear to have various and sometimes opposite movements, straight, curved, or circular, still the universe moves in harmony. Another example is the human body, of which each member has its different function, yet they work in unity toward the health of the body.[40] The Word also makes the body grow and the soul that possesses life and thought move. The Word of God, through his own power, moves both the visible world and the invisible powers.[41] When humans observe creation, employ their intelligence, and observe themselves, they discover art.[42] To produce art humans use the rational aspect of human

37. *C. Gent.* 42.

38. *C. Gent.* 41.

39. *C. Gent.* 42. Athanasius writes in *Orationes contra Arianos* II that the stars and the great lights all came into being by the same command at the same time and together form a unity in creation. *C. Ar.* 2.48. As the visible things were not created independent of each other but together and in harmony so were the invisible things. *C. Ar.* 2.49. When we observe creation filled with the knowledge of God and exhibiting the order and harmony of all things, we acknowledge the Maker and Lord of all things. *C. Ar.* 2.32.

40. *C. Gent.* 43.

41. *C. Gent.* 44.

42. *C. Gent.* 18.

nature, which reflects the image of God. Beyond its instructive power to inspire art, nature also reveals God, its creator.

God has given humanity a soul endowed with reason/*nous* to contemplate and to know God. Humans were immersed in their senses and desires and turned away from God. Their senses overtook their reason and they did not find God's presence in creation and did not recognize him as the creator but made creation their god and worshiped created objects. God would not let his creation go to waste and sent his Word, the only Begotten Son, to save humanity, thus the necessity of the incarnation.

THE INCARNATION, CRUCIFIXION, AND RESURRECTION

The text with the title *On the Incarnation* addresses three types of audiences: Jews, pagans/gentiles, and the faithful. Athanasius addresses each audience differently. God reveals himself to humanity in different forms: through the human *nous*/reason, through creation, and through Scripture. Athanasius addresses the Jews through Scripture, the pagans/gentiles through reason, and the faithful by explaining that God revealed himself to humanity through the incarnation. God reveals himself to all humanity in the way that suits each person best.

Athanasius demonstrates to the Jews that Old Testament prophecies are fulfilled in Jesus Christ; he is the expected Messiah. For example: Isaiah 7:14 was fulfilled with the birth of Christ from the Virgin Mary, Isaiah 53 was fulfilled with the suffering and death of Christ on the cross, and Christ fulfilled Isaiah 35:5–6 with the miracles he performed. After a long list of fulfilled biblical prophecies, he concludes that prophecies and visions ceased in Israel after the coming of Christ, an indication that the coming

The Incarnation, Creation, and Renewal

of Christ fulfilled all the prophecies.[43] Athanasius interprets the Old Testament typologically: Old Testament prophecies are types pointing to Christ's incarnation and his work within humanity.

The gentiles are versed in philosophy and are familiar with the concept of the *logos*. Athanasius addresses the Gentiles by arguing that, if the Logos fills the whole body of the world, it can also be in a human body, which is part of the body of the world. The Logos is not diminished by dwelling in a human body just as the human mind is not diminished in its being when expressed by the tongue.[44] In addition, Athanasius argues that God's knowledge fills the earth,[45] and humanity can see God in the heavenly order and see the Logos's power through his works. The Logos destroyed death through the resurrection and changed the nature of water at Cana of Galilee. The Logos touched all creation to free humanity from its illusions so that it can worship Christ and through him come to know the Father. The incarnation transformed humanity. The faith in the resurrection and immortality changed and empowered humanity to get rid of its violent nature, to observe the virtue of chastity, overcome the fear of death and martyrdom, and live the life of self-restraint and virtue of the soul.[46] Athanasius addressed the gentiles through reason, knowledge, and creation.

Athanasius takes a theological approach when he addresses the Christians. He begins his treatise with the creation narrative. God created all things through the Word, the incorporeal Son of God; therefore, it is consistent for the Father to renew the world through the Word who made

43. *Inc.* 33–40.
44. *Inc.* 41–42.
45. Isa 11:9.
46. *Inc.* 43–53.

it from the beginning. The Son had to be incarnate. God manifested his Son to us because of the lovingkindness of the Father and for the sake of our salvation.[47] When God created humans, he gave them the gift of being made in his own image and having a portion of the power of his own Word; being made rational, thus being a reflection of the Word, they live a life of blessedness. God created humanity with the grace of free will. God secured their free will with a law through which, if they kept it, they would remain in paradise without sorrow or pain. If they transgressed the law, they would suffer corruption in their nature and die. This was the commandment: "And the LORD God commanded the man, 'You may freely eat of every tree of the garden; but of the tree of the knowledge of good and evil you shall not eat, for in the day that you eat of it you shall die.'"[48] Humanity transgressed the commandment; humans turned away from God, and suffered death and corruption.[49]

Humanity was created out of nothing. As the consequences of the transgression humans died, suffered corruption, and were reduced to nothing; they were reduced to what is not. For evil is what is not and what is good is. When humans rejected the contemplation of God, they turned away from God to what was not. Humans are mortal in nature, but if they had preserved God's knowledge within them, if they had preserved his image and likeness, they would have become incorrupt and immortal. The Book of Wisdom says: "Giving heed to her [wisdom's] laws is

47. *Inc.* 1, 10.

48. Gen 2:16–17; *Inc.* 3.

49. Athanasius intentionally uses the term *parabasis*, meaning "an overstepping, deviation, or transgression" and not the term *hamartia*, meaning "fault, failure, guilt, or sin." For at this moment in history, humanity transgressed the commandment and ate from the tree of knowledge. See Liddell et al., *Greek-English Lexicon*, s.v. *parabasis* and *hamartia*.

The Incarnation, Creation, and Renewal

assurance of immortality."[50] Those who are immortal live as God, for Scripture says: "I say, 'You are gods, children of the Most High, all of you; nevertheless, you shall die like mortals, and fall like any prince.'"[51] Those who preserve God's knowledge, image, and likeness will become immortal, thus be a god and a child of the Most High. This is at the core of the concept of *theopoiēsis*, to be made divine, which will be discussed in detail in chapter 5.

When death took hold of the rational humanity made in the image of God, humans began to perish. God gave a command with a consequence, if they transgress it they die, and God's word has to be true, so humans have to die.[52] If God accepted repentance as a solution for transgression, humanity would remain in its corruptible state forever. God's lovingkindness would not let humanity perish, so the Father sent the Word to recreate and renew everything and overcome death and corruption. Thus the necessity of the incarnation.[53]

The incarnation did not change the essence of the incorporeal and incorruptible Word of God; he is always with the Father, filling creation, and present everywhere.[54] The incarnation did not contain him nor bind him to his body, but rather he contained all things within himself. While in the body, he quickened his own body, quickened the whole universe, and was dwelling with his Father.[55] The incorporeal and incorruptible Word of God took a body and made it his own (*idiopoieitai*).[56] He took a body like

50. Wis 6:18.
51. Ps 82:6–7; *Inc.* 4.
52. *Inc.* 6.
53. *Inc.* 7.
54. *Inc.* 8.
55. *Inc.* 17.
56. *Inc.* 8. Thomson, *Contra gentes and De incarnatione*, 152.

ours, and when in his lovingkindness he died on the cross we all died in him; on behalf of all he overcome death and corruption. When he made the body his own, by the grace of the resurrection overcoming death and incorruption, he granted life and renewal to all of humanity.[57] Now death has no hold over humanity.[58]

Athanasius holds that the Logos become incarnate not only to overcome death and grant us eternal life but also to reveal himself and the Father to humanity. When humanity did not recognize God through creation and did not

---

See also Thomson, *Contra gentes and De incarnatione*, 175, 210 (*idiopoiēsato*); *C. Ar.* 3.33; *Ep. Epict.* 6; and Cyril of Alexandria, *Anathema* 2. The term "makes it his own" (*idiopoieitai*) or just "his own" (*to idios*) becomes a technical theological term and a signature Athanasian term that defines his understanding of the relationship of the flesh to the incarnate Logos. Chapter 8 of *De incarnatione*, as well as a few other places in the text add to the body that is "his own" the expression "as an instrument." Most Greek manuscripts add that the Word took a body as his own "as an instrument." I argue, based on textual and theological evidence and its theological reception, especially by Cyril of Alexandria, that "as an instrument" is a textual interpolation as it contradicts Athanasius's theology. In *Contra Arianos*, Athanasius established that, for the Incarnate Logos to overcome corruption and death, he had to take a body and make it "his own" so that the properties and the suffering of the flesh are also said to be his own. If the Incarnate Logos is external to this suffering he cannot overcome death and corruption for the sake of humanity. In *De incarnatione*, Athanasius insists that the body must be "his own" or else the body will only appear as in a theophany; therefore the Logos must assert the body is "his own" and not use it as an instrument, or an apparition, or other external manifestation as some Docetists might claim. In the second context of *De incarnatione* he explains to the Greeks the necessity of the incarnation: it is only through the body, part of the whole, not external to the whole, that overcoming death and corruption is accomplished. If corruption and death are not external to the body, then the body cannot be external to the Logos. Farag, "*Organon*," 93–105.

57. *Inc.* 8.
58. *Inc.* 9.

The Incarnation, Creation, and Renewal

understand God revealing himself to humanity through the law and prophets, then the incarnation became a necessity.[59] The Word (*logos/reason*) of the Father created humanity with rationality that it might know God. For why would God create humans if they were not to know him? He creates humanity in his own image and after his likeness, so that by perceiving the image, the Logos, humans may know the Father and their creator and live a blessed life. When humans rejected God, their souls were darkened and they forgot God and became consumed with themselves, their desires, and the work of lawlessness. God became unknown to humanity. When the incarnate Logos sacrificed his body, the body that is his own, on the cross, he put an end to the law against humanity, and by his resurrection we have a new life, a life of renewal. Just as through man death prevailed over humanity, by the Logos who became incarnate death was destroyed and through the resurrection humanity received eternal life.[60]

One aspect of the renewal granted by the resurrection is the renewal of the divine image within humanity. Not even angels can renew humanity—it had to be the Word of God, the Image of the Father; only he could recover and renew the divine image in humanity.[61] At this point, Athanasius gives more details about his understanding of renewal: The soul is "born and created anew in the likeness of God's image." Since the mind is a part of the soul, so the renewal of the soul renews the mind (*nous*) through which humanity is able to know God.[62] By means of the signs and works done by the body that is his own, the incarnate Logos revealed himself, humanity got to know the Word of

---

59. *Inc.* 12.
60. *Inc.* 10–11.
61. *Inc.* 13.
62. *Inc.* 14.

God and through him know the Father.[63] He is not only Son of Man but also God the Word who manifested himself through works of love and overcame death and renewed humanity.[64] When the Gospels say that the incarnate Logos was born, that his body was sustained by food, and that he suffered in the body, it is to assert his full humanity and to vanquish any claims of later Docetism. The Gospels also proclaim his works, his miracles of healing, changing the substance of water into wine, walking on the water, and feeding the multitudes, thus affirming that he is the Son of God.[65] Creation also proclaimed him as Son of God: when it witnessed his death on the cross, the earth quaked and there was darkness as the sun hid its light at the sight of its crucified creator.[66]

The death of the incarnate Son on the cross on our behalf has given humanity immortality and incorruption. When the incarnate Son died, his body did not see corruption, for he rose again in a perfect state, for he was Life and his body belonged to Life itself. The resurrection of Christ was the moment of victory over death and corruption. When we die now, our bodies dissolve and see corruption, waiting to rise again in incorruption at the time of the final resurrection. His resurrection guaranteed the incorruption of our bodies at the time of the final resurrection.[67] Athanasius returns to the theme of martyrdom to confirm that the power of Christ's victory over death and faith in the incorruptibility of humanity after the final resurrection are what empowered the martyrs to face death without fear. Their death was a testimony to such theology and was the

63. *Inc.* 14.
64. *Inc.* 16.
65. *Inc.* 18.
66. *Inc.* 26, 19.
67. *Inc.* 21, 22, 26, 27.

means by which those who witnessed their heroic, fearless death came to the faith that death is not destruction but the beginning of a life of incorruption.[68] The resurrection gave humanity immortality, virtue, desire for the heavenly things, and knowledge of the Father. It overcame death, revealed the Word, displaced idolatry, and revealed the power of the cross over all evil powers. In addition, the resurrection made humanity look away from earthly matters to the heavenly. The Son never ceases to work "for the Son of God is living and active."[69]

In *Against the Gentiles* and *On the Incarnation* Athanasius lays out his theological understanding of the incarnation and the power of the resurrection in our lives. He begins with the creation narrative. God created humanity in his image and likeness through the Word/Logos. He endowed humanity with reason/rationale/*nous* to know God our creator and to guide us in our lives. It is this endowed reason that gives us free will, makes us distinct from the rest of creation, and makes us be in his image and after his likeness. When we transgressed his commandment by our own free will, we lost God's image within us, death had power over us, and we suffered corruptibility. God in his

---

68. *Inc.* 27, 28, 29. Athanasius elaborates on the theme of martyrdom, writing that martyrs believed that they were passing to life rather than undergoing death. The incarnate Logos took a body as his own and faced death on the cross and abolished death by death. By facing this terror he removed our terror and thus humans are not to fear death; he took away our terror. Humans die by force of nature against their will, but the incarnate Logos, being immortal while having a mortal flesh, had the power as God to raise his own body; the corruptible became incorruptible. We no longer remain mortal because the Word has assumed our mortality; we partake of immortality that is from him. *C. Ar.* 3.56. Thus, Christians face death without fear because they are attaining life and immortality through Christ who overcame death and mortality.

69. *Inc.* 31.

lovingkindness would not leave us to return to non-existence, for this is what death means; we came from nothing and we return to nothing. He sent his Son, who took a body as his own, so that through his body that encompasses all that humanity he would overcome death by his resurrection and renew our human nature. Through the body that is his own he took all that belonged to us, corruption and death, and with the power of his resurrection overcame death and gave us the life of incorruptibility. In the beginning we were created in his image and after his likeness and endowed with reason/*nous*, but we were liable to corruption like the rest of creation if we transgressed the commandment. After the resurrection, humanity was granted incorruptibility, something that the rest of creation never had. Incorruptibility and eternity is part of the divine essence. Athanasius summarized his theology of the incarnation in his famous dictum, God "became human, so that we might be made divine (*theopoiēthōmen*)."[70] God became incarnate so that we would regain the divine image within us, become renewed, and so that our human trait of corruptibility would be made incorruptible, a divine attribute that humanity never had.

Athanasius believes that theology is not an intellectual exercise confined to metaphysical speculations but relates to our everyday life and spirituality. He concludes the treatise *On the Incarnation* by saying that an honorable life, a pure soul, and a life of virtue are needed to understand and know Scriptures. The *nous* guides the soul to attain its desire and knowledge of the Word of God. Humanity can understand Scripture, which pertains to God and his Word, with a pure mind and a saintly and holy life.[71] A holy life renewed by the resurrection and leading to the knowledge of God might seem unattainable to the average Christian.

70. *Inc.* 54.
71. *Inc.* 57.

The Incarnation, Creation, and Renewal

Athanasius points to a certain Antony, who lived an ascetic life in the desert of Egypt and attained such a renewed life. Antony is an example of a person who lived in deep contemplation on Scripture accompanied by a holy and saintly life and reached the knowledge of God as far as humans can. The *Life of Antony* demonstrates this theology in practice. It is a detailed practical account of the struggles of the mind and soul to attain the renewed life.

ANTONY, AN EXEMPLAR OF THE LIFE OF RENEWAL[72]

Athanasius explains in his introductory paragraph of the *Life of Antony*, that "the name 'monk' designates a way of life." He describes the life of Antony and monasticism as a "way of life" (*politeia*) not a set of rules.[73] Athanasius reminds the reader that they will "marvel" at Antony's *politeia* but at the same time he cautions them that he did not write *Life* to engender skepticism but as an example to aspire to and to emulate.

The *Life* informs us that Antony responded to a call from Scripture. After the death of his parents, Antony entered the church reflecting on what to do with his life and his newly inherited wealth. The gospel messages on two Sundays were Matthew 19:21 and 6:34, which call for perfection in the Christian life and renouncing one's

72. For a detailed discussion of Antony as a model of life of renewal read, Farag, *Balance*, 47–94. There is some debate about the attribution of the *Life of Antony* to Athanasius, but for the purpose of this book, the attribution to Athanasius will be accepted. For more references about the debates see Leemans, "Thirteen Years," 153–59. For a survey of the authenticity of the *Life of Antony* see Ernest, *Bible*, 435–36.

73. Athanasius, *Life of Anthony: The Coptic Life and The Greek Life*, 52; *Vit. Ant.*2.

possessions for the sake of the heavenly kingdom. Athanasius's argument that Scripture is a means of revelation and instruction to the *nous* that guides the soul is demonstrated in this event. These biblical messages guided Antony to renounce his newly acquired wealth and devote himself to deep prayer and self-reflection, seeking to be closer to God. Athanasius informs us that this process was gradual, even renouncing his possessions was incremental rather than all at once. He did not immediately move to the desert, but first moved outside his house, then to the outskirts of his village, and gradually to the inner desert, that is, far from the main caravan route or any trodden road. The spiritual growth within the narrative of the *Life of Antony* shows a gradual spiritual learning curve guided by the *nous* giving knowledge to the soul to act on things against its nature. That is the power of the resurrection and the renewal of humanity. While humans are prone to accumulation of wealth and seeking renown in their social milieu, Antony did the exact opposite: he relinquished his wealth and lived in seclusion to be forgotten by society but known to God alone. This is the paradox that for Athanasius was exemplified by the martyrs: humans are prone to self-preservation, but the Christians moved toward martyrdom, not fearing death because the resurrection overcame death. The resurrection empowered humanity to overcome all its fears and self-indulgence in wealth and material power. Antony represented the power of the resurrection and renewal in our lives.

Antony applied himself to learn from everyone. He learned patience from one and courage from another; he learned humility from one and prayer from others. This observant learning from everyone requires humility. He actively consulted and sought the advice of elders who had spiritual experience. Antony, as well as the monastics

The Incarnation, Creation, and Renewal

who followed his example, had another, and main, source of knowledge: Scripture. The *Life* describes the rhythm of monastic life as studying the Bible, praying and singing psalms, working and giving alms, loving each other and living in harmony. Antony would also reflect "in his heart on the heavenly dwellings."[74] Scripture was at the center of the spiritual life that Antony led, Scripture revealed God to him, and Scripture was the source of his prayers and psalms. This was combined with a life of reflection.

Athanasius describes a life centered on cultivating the *nous* to nourish and guide the soul. Scripture reveals God to Antony and is the main source of spiritual instruction. Seclusion calms the senses and uplifts Antony to contemplate creation and the heavenly realm rather than be driven by the senses and desires. Prayer and the singing of psalms are inspired by Scripture and nourish the *nous* that guides the soul to tranquility and further knowledge of God. All of this resulted in a life of renewal and inner transformation for Antony. Athanasius goes further to assert that the inner transformation was physically visible. Though nothing was distinguishable about Antony's physical appearance, people would come to him "as though drawn by his eyes" or his face.[75] "Because his soul was tranquil," Athanasius explains, "it produced for [him] imperturbable outer senses so that because of his joyful soul his face was filled with joy and from the movements of his body others perceived and understood the stability of quality of soul as it were, as it is written: 'A glad heart makes a cheerful countenance but it is sorrowful when there is sadness.'"[76] Antony's soul reflects

---

74. Athanasius, *Life of Anthony: The Coptic Life and The Greek Life*, 153; *Vit Ant.* 44.

75. Athanasius, *Life of Anthony: The Coptic Life and The Greek Life*, 200; *Vit Ant.* 67.

76. Prov 15:13; Athanasius, *Life of Anthony: The Coptic Life and*

the guidance of the *nous* and the fullness of renewal that inspired and transformed many surrounding him.

Antony delivers a long discourse to the monks that crystalizes the monastic thought guiding the *Life*.[77] Antony tells the monks that virtue "is within us and has its origin from us. Virtue comes into being because the soul naturally possesses the rational faculty of understanding."[78] Antony continues his discourse describing the soul: "The soul is 'straight' when its rational faculty of understanding is as it was created according to nature. On the other hand, when it bends and become twisted contrary to its nature, then we speak of the soul's evil."[79] Antony concludes that the life of virtue is not difficult because virtue is within us and we can protect ourselves from evil thoughts and preserve the soul as when God created it.[80] This is one aspect of the practical advice Antony gave his monks to live the life of virtue. It places the theology of the incarnation at the center of spiritual practice.

The trilogy of *Against the Gentiles*, *On the Incarnation*, and *Life of Antony* form one cohesive narrative of the incarnation, crucifixion, and resurrection. It begins with

---

The Greek Life, 200; *Vit. Ant.* 67.

77. The long discourse is in *Vit. Ant.* 16–43. Tim Vivian summarizes two opposing scholarly views about the *Life of Antony*: Bartelink suggests that the discourse represents Athanasius's point of view. See Bartelink, *Athanase d'Alexandrie*, 117n3. Rubenson defends the opinion that the discourse is very close to the Letters of Antony in style and content. See Rubenson, *Letters of St. Antony*, 40. From: Athanasius, *Life of Anthony: The Coptic Life and The Greek Life*, 97, xxiv–xxvii.

78. Athanasius, *Life of Anthony: The Coptic Life and The Greek Life*, 106; *Ant.* 20.

79. Athanasius, *Life of Anthony: The Coptic Life and The Greek Life*, 107; *Ant.* 20.

80. Athanasius, *Life of Anthony: The Coptic Life and The Greek Life*, 107; *Ant.* 20.

The Incarnation, Creation, and Renewal

the creation narrative and the status of humanity before the transgression of the commandment. Humanity used its free will and chose to follow its own desires and senses, and was swayed away from God. Humanity lost God's image and likeness and was under the grasp of death. God in his lovingkindness sent the Logos, the Word, through whom all things came to be, to renew humanity. The Son of God became incarnate, took a body that encompasses all that humanity is, and made it his own. With the crucifixion and resurrection he overcame death, renewed God's image and likeness, and granted immortality to humanity. God became human so that humanity might be made divine. The power of renewal is within us and guides the *nous* towards the life of virtue and choosing what is good, even if it sometimes contradicts the desires of the soul. The life of Antony is an example of how to overcome the desires that pull us away from God to live a life of blessedness guided by the soul that has knowledge of God through the *nous*.[81]

QUESTIONS FOR FURTHER DISCUSSION

- How did Athanasius explain the origin of evil? Give special attention to his understanding of the human person.
- How did Athanasius explain the incarnation and salvation? Is it different from other ancient and medieval western theologians' understanding of salvation?
- How did Athanasius describe the role of the soul and *nous* in the life of renewal?
- How did the *Life of Antony* contribute to the understanding of the life of renewal and spirituality?

---

81. For another summary of the theology of the Athanasian trilogy see Farag, *Balance*, 91–94.

SUGGESTIONS FOR FURTHER READING

Contra gentes and *On The Incarnation* (NPNF or Thomson translation)
With special attention to:
The soul: *Contra Gentes* 30–34
The origin of evil: *Contra Gentes* 1–7
Creation: *Contra Gentes* 35–45
On the Incarnation 1–32, 54–57
Life of Antony

3

SCRIPTURE

Scripture is at the center of Athanasius's theological thought and writings. His theology is biblically based and his biblical interpretation is theological and spiritual. Athanasius never wrote a biblical commentary, but he explicitly wrote about the theological method of interpretation as it informs theology and exposes Arian theological inconsistency and unorthodoxy. Attempts to work out his method of biblical interpretation depend primarily on his polemical writings. The Arian controversy shaped these writings, which are geared to proving that the Arians misinterpreted biblical verses. Aspects of his methodology are influenced by this context. It is important to give attention to Athanasius's interpretative method since it shaped and defined the theology of the universal church; it is this method which asserted the divinity of the Son as well as that of the Holy Spirit. This chapter begins with general observations about the role of Scripture, both Old and New Testaments, in

Athanasius's writings, then examines his methods of interpretation, that is, his theological and spiritual interpretations. This chapter is a short introduction to these themes as the following chapters provide further examples in context.

INTRODUCTORY OBSERVATIONS

Festal Letter 39, written in 367, demonstrates the centrality of Scripture in Athanasius's work. The letter provides a list of the canonical Old and New Testament books accepted in the Alexandrian Church. The books of the New Testament canon listed in this letter are the same as the ones used in our present day Bibles. Athanasius mentions in the letter that some use "fabricated" books to advance their teachings and mislead the simple. Athanasius found it necessary to address this problem in his festal letter and prescribe the books that lay the foundation upon which churches can begin theological discussions. Scripture is the yardstick upon which Athanasius judges the orthodoxy of any teaching and securing the canonical books is a means to secure the orthodoxy of the faith.

In his *Letter to the Bishops of Egypt and Libya* Athanasius exhorts the faithful Christians who are true disciples of the Gospel and have the grace to discern spiritual things to be aware of deceitful teachings. However lengthy his discourse might be, Scripture is "most sufficient"; any knowledge they want to acquire they will find in Scripture.[1] His belief that a Christian is a disciple of the Gospel and that Scripture is at the center of Christian knowledge sheds light on the role of Scripture in Athanasius's thought.

Athanasius also urges those who read and exegete Scripture to interpret verses in context and not ignore parts of Scripture. For example, Hebrews 3:2a says that Jesus "was

---

1. *Ep. Aeg. Lib.* 4.

faithful to the one made him (*tō poiēsanti auton*)." When taken out of context, which is how the Arians interpreted it, it would mean the Son is a created being made (*epoieēse*) by the Father. Athanasius explains that the Apostle is addressing the Son who became incarnate, so that his humanity—the Word took earthly flesh—is what was "made" or created. Further, in his capacity as incarnate Son, the term "made" takes on the sense of appointed as an apostle and high priest, just as Moses was "made" or "appointed" over God's house.[2] The context that the Arians missed was that this verse is not addressing the Son in his divinity but rather the incarnate Son, who is both human and divine at the same time.

Ecclesiastes 12:14, "God shall bring every work (*poiēma*) into judgment," provides another example of Arians interpreting a text out of context and not taking into consideration the multiple senses of the term *poiēma*. The Arians considered the Word to be a created being and therefore a "work" of God who will stand judgment. The Arian argument follows Hebrews 3:1, which describes Jesus as faithful to God, and connects it with Ecclesiastes where all "works," that is the "faithful," will stand judgment. Therefore, the Arians concluded that Jesus will stand judgment. Athanasius asks how the judge will be on trial. What law will judge the Lawgiver? Athanasius begins his argument by saying that God is faithful and true.[3] In addition, Paul writes that God is faithful and will not test anyone beyond

---

2. *C. Ar.* 2. 7. It should be noted that the NRSV has taken this theological argument into account and translated the verse as follows: "consider that Jesus, the apostle and high priest of our confession, was faithful to the one who appointed (ποιήσαντι) him, just as Moses also 'was faithful in all God's house'" (Heb 3:1, 2, NRSV).

3. Deut 32:4; Exod 34:6; Rev 3:14.

their strength.⁴ Athanasius concludes there are two senses for the term "faithful" in Scripture, the first is "believing" and the second is "trustworthy," of which the former belongs to humans and the latter belongs to God. Thus, Abraham was faithful because he believed in God's word, and when David gives praise, saying "the Lord is faithful in all his words,"⁵ he means God is trustworthy and does not lie.⁶ In conclusion, the Son is not a work and does not stand in judgment before God. This is another aspect of Athanasius's method of interpreting verses, and words within verses, in context; thus, to understand the meaning of a specific term, such as "faithful," one must examine it to see if it is applied to God or to humanity.

The previous two examples are theological interpretations. This is Athanasius's primary method of interpretation. In these examples Athanasius demonstrates two principles of interpretation: interpret verses first within their immediate context and then within the larger context of scripture, including both Old and New Testaments. Theological interpretation has shaped the way we interpret and read Scripture to this day and affects our present-day biblical translations. In the previous two examples, the interpretations are based on the Greek text in which the Greek words for "made" and "faithful" carry several meanings and nuances. The theologically accepted meaning was settled through Athanasius's theological interpretation centuries ago and modern translations follow the Nicene and

---

4. 1 Cor 10:13.

5. Ps 145:13.

6. *C. Ar.* 2.6. Again observe how modern translation has taken such theological interpretation into consideration: "For God will bring every deed into judgment, including every secret thing, whether good or evil" (Eccl 12:14, NRSV).

Athanasian argument as demonstrated above (see notes 2 and 6).

The Septuagint (LXX) was the Scripture of the Early Church and Athanasius uses it for his reading and interpretation. The LXX had some translation problems that affected the Arian debate; a good example is Prov 8:22, "The LORD created me [wisdom] at the beginning of his work, the first of his acts of long ago." The problem is the word "created." This was one of the key verses that the Arians used to argue that the Son is "created" and thus a creature and not divine. Athanasius uses sections 18–82 of the second *Oration against the Arians*, that is, most of the *Second Oration*, to interpret Prov 8:22 in a way that defends the divinity of the Son. If Athanasius knew Hebrew, like his fellow Alexandrian, Origen, in the previous century, the problem would be solved as the Hebrew word *qānā* (קָנָנִי קָנָה) means "acquire," "buy," "buy as wife," or "ransom"; "acquire wisdom" would have solved the problem since no reference to creation is made. The LXX translators translated the Hebrew *qānā* by the Greek *ektisen* (ἔκτισέν) meaning "created." Few early Christian writers referred to the Hebrew text and when Arius raised this issue arguing that the Son was created, Athanasius, like other early Christian theologians, argued on theological not linguistic bases, not referring to the Hebrew original. The interpretation of Proverbs 8:22 is the most difficult and lengthy argument in the whole of the *Oration against the Arians*. Arius argues that the "me" in "The LORD created me at the beginning of his work" in Prov 8:22 refers to the Son who is a created being and thus not fully divine. Athanasius responds that "me" refers to Wisdom, for Wisdom built itself a house.[7] The house of Wisdom refers to created humanity through which the Word and Wisdom became human, for as John

---

7. Prov 9:1.

wrote, "the Word became flesh."[8] Athanasius emphasizes that what is "created" is not the essence of the Godhead but the humanity of the incarnate Word. Athanasius adds that Proverbs should not be interpreted in a literal sense but as what they are, proverbs.[9] Athanasius explains that "He created" does not refer to the essence and mode of generation but sometimes means "renewal" as in "create in me a clean heart."[10] Athanasius reminds his readers that to be called creatures indicates things have by nature a created essence. Athanasius accuses Arius of inconsistency for allegorizing the "house" in Proverbs 9:1, where Wisdom has built her house and set up her seven pillars, but insisting on taking Proverbs 8:22 literally and holding that the Son is a created being.

Athanasius explains that misinterpretation of biblical passages arises when one does not consider the *skopos* of the faith.[11] Athanasius distinguishes between interpretation according to the accepted catholic faith of the church, accepted by the church as a body as represented in the Council of Nicaea, and private interpretation which starts with "I believe," representing personal interpretations, which are a novelty, not representing the accepted faith or tradition.[12] Athanasius reasons that the faith Christians hold should be used as a rule: when the rule is applied to the reading of Scripture we interpret Scripture according to the faith.[13] Athanasius accuses the Arians of misinterpreting Scripture according to their private sense. The purpose for writing

8. John 1:14.
9. *C. Ar.* 2.44–45.
10. Ps 51:10.
11. *Skopos* means the object on which one fixes the eye, a mark, or an aim, end. See Liddell et al., *Greek-English Lexicon*, s.v. σκοπός.
12. *Syn.* 3–4.
13. *C. Ar.* 3.28.

Scripture

the three *Orations against the Arians* was to expose the Arian private interpretations that were against the orthodox sense.[14] Athanasius explains the source of orthodoxy is tradition embodied in the sound faith that Christ gave us, which the Apostles preached, which was handed down to the church and the Fathers who came from all over the world to meet at Nicaea.[15] He adds that the orthodoxy of the faith starts with the teachings of the Apostles, which was handed down by the Fathers, and confirmed by both the Old and New Testaments.[16] Athanasius considers the Council of Nicaea to be a cornerstone of the Christian faith whose teachings are held to be equal to those of the Apostles. One of the guiding rules Athanasius establishes then is that it consider the *skopos* of the faith and not contradict the faith established by tradition exemplified in Christ, the Old and New Testaments, the Apostles, the Fathers, and the Council of Nicaea.

Athanasius affirms the use of the Old Testament in opposition to Marcion and Mani. Athanasius argues that the New Testament arose out of the Old Testament and bears witness to it for it is the fulfillment of God's promises. It is only through Scripture that we can confess the Lord. If we reject the Old Testament, how can we accept the one of whom Moses and the Prophets wrote? It is through the Law that we came to know of the coming of Christ, who is both Lord of the Law and the Prophets. If we deny one, we deny the other.[17]

Athanasius cites the New Testament twice as much as the Old Testament. The book he quotes most from the Old Testament is the book of Psalms, followed by Proverbs and

14. *C. Ar.* 1.37.
15. *Ep. Afr.* 1.
16. *Ep. Adelph.* 6.
17. *Ep. Aeg. Lib.* 4.

Isaiah. Of the Gospels, he uses John and Matthew the most, followed by Luke; of the Epistles, Romans, Hebrews, and 1 Corinthians are used most.[18] This general observation tells us that Athanasius did not neglect use of the Old Testament and his theology is more heavily dependent on the Gospel narrative than the Pauline and other epistles. The theological prominence of the Gospel narrative, especially that of John, is a distinctive trait in Alexandrian theology.[19]

METHODS OF INTERPRETATION

Athanasius interweaves scriptural verses throughout his polemical writings. Non-polemical texts such as *Against the Gentiles*, *On The Incarnation*, or *Life of Antony* include scriptural verses but not in the same intensively interwoven fashion as the polemical. The method of weaving scriptural verses throughout his argument is based on his understanding that the scope of his theology should be inspired by Scripture, for the Lord himself said, "Search the Scriptures for they testify of me."[20] The following example is one of many that clarify the method Athanasius uses. Athanasius accuses the Arians who deny the divinity of the Son of fighting the Godhead itself, who proclaimed "this is my Son" with the understanding that the Son is of the same substance as the Father. A thread of verses forming a full paragraph follows, each showing the Father declaring the Son's divinity. Athanasius begins with Proverbs 8:25, in which God speaks about the Son being begotten not

---

18. I used the indices of the NPNF and Ernest.

19. Cyril of Alexandria, the inheritor of the Athanasian theological heritage, will build on and develop Athanasius's theology and will preserve the Johanine emphasis. See Farag, *St. Cyril of Alexandria*.

20. *C. Ar.* 3.29; John 5:39.

created.[21] The Arians do not trust the Scripture that proclaims that the Son is the brightness of God's glory and the exact representation of his *hypostasis*, and the power and wisdom of God.[22] He then weaves his argument with more Old Testament verses that clearly refer to divine aspects of the Son: he is the well of life, we see light with his light, and all things are made in wisdom.[23] "The Word of the Lord came to me, and thus declared," that "In the beginning was the Word."[24] Athanasius follows this with the idea of the Word delivered to us, as found in Jeremiah, John, and, finally, in Luke, "handed on to us by those who from the beginning were eyewitnesses and servants of the word."[25] Further still, "God sent his Word and we were healed."[26] For Athanasius these verses signify the eternity of the Word and of the *hypostasis*, or substance, of the Father. This line of argument is one example of many that demonstrates how Athanasius weaves scriptural verses to substantiate his theological stance. He also uses verses to give flavor to his arguments or express his attitude towards his opponents: for example, he denounces the Arians for fighting against the divinity with "a tongue as sharp as a sword."[27]

The most important method of theological interpretation that Athanasius follows is based on the principle of the "double accounts." Athanasius wrote about the double accounts:

21. Prov 8:25, LXX: "before all hills, he begets [*genna*] me."
22. Heb 1:3; 1 Cor 1:24.
23. Pss 36:9; 104:24; Jer 2:1.
24. Jer 2:1; John 1:1.
25. Luke 1:2.
26. Ps 107:20.
27. Ps 57:4.

> Now the scope and character of Holy Scripture, as we have often said, is this, it contains a double account of the Savior; that He was ever God, and is the Son, being the Father's Word and Radiance and Wisdom; and that afterwards for us He took flesh of a Virgin, Mary, Bearer of God, and was made man. And this scope is to be found throughout inspired Scriptures, for they are they which testify of Me.[28]

The double accounts principle of interpretation was crucial during the Arian controversy as Arius focused on the accounts pertaining to the humanity of the incarnate Son and deduced that the Son was a creature. Athanasius introduces the method of the double accounts to show that Arius's conclusions were wrong. Athanasius elaborates on the above quotation, starting with the opening of John's gospel: "In the beginning was the Word, and the Word was with God, and the Word was God. He was in the beginning with God,"[29] which is followed by "And the Word became flesh and lived among us, and we have seen his glory, a glory as of a father's only son, full of grace and truth."[30] John in his introductory narrative moves from the beginning of the Word with God, declaring the divinity, to the Word become flesh, revealing the economy and the humanity, in one consistent narrative. Athanasius next turns to Paul, who wrote that Christ, "though he was in the form of God, did not regard equality with God as something to be exploited, but emptied himself, taking the form of a slave, being born in human likeness. And being found in human form, he humbled himself

---

28. *C. Ar.* 3.29. John 5:39. The term *Theotokos* is usually rendered as "Bearer of God." Quotes are from the NPNF edition, unless otherwise noted.

29. John 1:1.

30. John 1:14.

Scripture

and became obedient to the point of death—even death on a cross."[31] Paul also speaks of both the form of God and the form of slave, the divinity and the humanity, in the same narrative. Athanasius thus shows the pattern and the movement from divinity to humanity and vice versa, within the same narrative. One can go through the rest of Scripture following this method of interpretation.[32]

The following example demonstrates how Athanasius applied the method of the double accounts in interpretation. Athanasius argues that when Proverbs 8:22 says "He created me," it refers to the Son who "put on created flesh." On the one hand, he is Word of the Father and calls God Father; on the other hand, he has taken the form of the servant and calls God Lord. Christ himself has taught us this difference, for he says, "I thank thee, O Father" and then "Lord of heaven and earth."[33] Christ calls God Father but when it is the creatures who address God, then God is addressed as Lord.[34] Athanasius furthers the discussion by asserting that Proverbs 8:22 does not refer to the essence of the Word but his humanity and his economy.[35] The verse emphasizes the Word was created "for his works" as coming second to his essence. Adam was created, not to work, but primarily to be a human being; later he received the command that he should work. Noah was created, not for the Ark, but received the commandment to build the Ark later. Similarly, Moses was created and then later was entrusted to govern the people. In each example, creation came first and the command to work came later. The Word was first,

31. Phil 2:6–8.
32. *C. Ar.* 3 29.
33. Matt 11:25.
34. *C. Ar.* 2.50.
35. The LXX translation of Prov 8:22: "The Lord made/created me the beginning of his ways for his works."

then, when creation needed restoration through the Word, the Word took it on himself to condescend and assimilate to the works, or created beings, which are referred to by the "he created." And this is confirmed by Isaiah 49:5: "Thus saith the Lord that formed me from the womb to be his own servant" (LXX).[36] Throughout this lengthy discussion, Athanasius asserts the principle that some accounts refer to the humanity and others refer to the divinity. Once the Arian controversy fades, the strong emphasis on the created aspect of the incarnate Son will not be part of the theological vocabulary. The argument moves beyond these concerns to the explanation of the nature of the incarnate Son, which will be picked up by Cyril of Alexandria.[37]

Athanasius furthers the discussion by explaining the differences in expression in the double accounts. Terms like "he created," "he formed," or "he set" refer to the economy that took place for the renewal of humanity and do not refer to the essence or the beginning of the Word. Scripture refers

---

36. *C. Ar.* 2.51.

37. Athanasius's double account does not imply the *communicatio idiomatum* (exchange of properties) principle necessitated by the two-nature Christology. Athanasius is defending the fullness of divinity of the Son both before and after the incarnation. To defend the fullness of divinity of the Son before the incarnation he emphasizes that the Son is not a created being against the assertions of the Arians. To defend the divinity of the Son after the incarnation he emphasizes the fullness of humanity of the incarnate Son with all its human attributes, except sin, so that all human attributes of Christ in the biblical narrative pertain to the humanity of the incarnate Son and are not attributes of the divinity. Once the divinity of the Son was confirmed in the Council of Nicaea and the aftermath of the Council, emphasis on the created humanity to affirm the divinity receded to the background. Athanasius is defending the essence and nature of the divinity of the Son. The *communicatio idiomatum* principle explains that the properties of each nature of the incarnate Son can be appropriated by the other. Athanasius is arguing for the divine essence, not the divine properties.

to his divinity in absolute terms without qualification, with no reason or purpose added. For example, when John 1:1 says "In the beginning was the Word, and the Word was with God, and the Word was God. He was in the beginning with God," no purpose is given. This verse refers to the divinity of the Son as it speaks in simple, absolute terms. By contrast, when John 1:14 says that "the Word became flesh," it immediately adds the purpose: "and dwelt among us," he became flesh for the sake of the economy. In Philippians 2:6–8, he "was in the form of God" is not followed by any purpose, but "he took the form of a slave" for our sake, to die on the cross. The purpose for his humility and incarnation pertains to his humanity and is for the economy.[38]

Athanasius uses the Holy Spirit as another important illustration of when texts should be read according to whether they are written in absolute or qualified form. Athanasius explains that when the Holy Spirit is mentioned in Scripture it is always qualified with a definite article or with "of God," "of the Father," "my," "his," "of Christ," "of the Son," "from me," referring to God, or "of Truth," referring to the Son who is the Truth. The Holy Spirit could also be mentioned in absolute terms by name: "the Holy Spirit" or "Paraclete." When the term "spirit" is written without qualification, it refers simply to a spirit but not the Holy Spirit.[39] Athanasius used this argument to oppose claims that spirit refers to angels, to which Athanasius responded that the Holy Spirit is always qualified as in "Spirit of adopted sonship," "Spirit of sanctification," "Spirit of God," and "Spirit of Christ."[40] Interpreting Scripture based on the close reading

38. *C. Ar.* 2.53.

39. *Ep. Serap.* 1.4.1. The translation of DelCogliano and Radde-Gallwitz unless otherwise noted.

40. *Ep. Serap.* 1.11.1. Rom 8:15; 1:4; 8:9; Matt 3:17; and 1 Pet 1:11. The translation of DelCogliano and Radde-Gallwitz.

of texts and terms had a far-reaching effect on theological understanding of the divine nature of Christ and the Holy Spirit.

Athanasius briefly touches on the idea that Scripture sometimes speaks not in a plain sense but in a hidden sense, in enigma. The book of Proverbs says "The Lord created me" not in the plain sense, for the Word never called himself a creature by nature, but in a hidden way; when we take away the veil we understand the hidden meaning and lay bare the enigma. Proverbs 1:5–6 says that a wise person of understanding will understand proverbs, figures, their interpretation, the words of the wise and their riddles.[41] Unveiling and understanding the hidden sense requires reading Scripture with wisdom.

Athanasius gives other examples of reading Scripture beyond the literal sense. Scripture uses images and illustrations from nature to demonstrate moral lessons for humanity. It uses images to demonstrate bad conduct, as when Christ exposed Herod and addressed him as "that fox."[42] Or when it gives this advice, "Do not be like a horse or a mule, without understanding, whose temper must be curbed."[43] Similarly, when Christ sent his disciples, he said "See, I am sending you out like sheep into the midst of wolves; so be wise as serpents and innocent as doves."[44] We are not instructed to become beasts of burden, Athanasius argues, but rather to understand the wisdom of one, the deception of another, or the meekness of a third.[45] These moral lessons were conveyed in images of nature familiar

---

41. *C. Ar.* 2.77. See also *C. Ar.* 2.44 for a more detailed explanation of not reading the plain sense of Prov 8:22.

42. Luke 13:32.

43. Ps 32:9.

44. Matt 10:16.

45. *C. Ar.* 3.18.

Scripture

to the audience, who would understand the meaning of the images conveyed. Athanasius gives a general assessment of Arius's biblical interpretation as missing the "right sense." For the Arians struggle with passages such as "The Lord created me," "Made better than the angels," or "First-born" because they thought God was material and interpreted immaterial things in a material way.[46]

The example of Matthew 12:40 deserves some attention: "For just as Jonah was three days and three nights in the belly of the sea monster, so for three days and three nights the Son of Man will be in the heart of the earth." Athanasius writes that Jonah was not the Savior, nor did he go to hades, nor was the whale hades, nor did Jonah bring up any other person from the belly of the whale except himself. "Therefore there is no identity nor equality signified in the term 'as,' but one thing and another; and it shows a certain kind of parallel in the case of Jonah, on account of the three days."[47] Similarly, when we become one as the Father and the Son are one, we become one in mind and agreement of spirit. We shall not be as the Son or equal to him for in our case "as" (*kathōs*) means parallel. For we are not of the same nature as the Son. The Son is in the Father by nature but for us it is an image or example. Redeemed humanity is no longer dead, but were made "as" (*kathōs*) God. We are not of God's nature and therefore do not actually become divine, but "as" (*kathōs*) the Son redeemed us through the incarnation and taking our humanity renewed and perfected his work, that is our humanity, we are made God (*theopoiēsis*).[48] *Theopoiēsis* does not make us gods, equal to God, or of his nature. The verb *poieō* and the term *poiēsis* indicate that the process of making divine is

46. *C. Ar.* 3.1.
47. *C. Ar.* 3.23.
48. *C. Ar.* 3.23.

related to created beings who are not of the nature of God. Athanasius's complex method of interpretation has a theological dimension and requires that attention be paid to the theological significance of words.

Athanasius interprets the Old Testament as a shadow and type of the New Testament. According to Athanasius, the example of Aaron being made a high priest was a shadow according to the Law. As Aaron did not change when he was "made" or "became" a high priest and was vested to perform his priestly functions, so the incarnation of the Son of God did not effect change in his divinity when he "became" human to accomplish our salvation.[49] Athanasius used shadow or type not only for polemical theological interpretation but also in his *Festal Letters*, which have a more pastoral dimension. *Festal Letter* 45 describes Moses making the tabernacle according to the pattern shown on the mount, so that the services were a type of the heavenly mysteries, and applies it to Easter: "As all the old things were a type of the new, so the festival that now is, is a type of the joy which is above."[50] Athanasius urges his listeners to celebrate Easter with great joy as it is a type of the heavenly joy we will experience in the heavenly kingdom.

THEOLOGICAL INTERPRETATION

Athanasius incorporates these approaches to Scripture into his theological interpretation, as when he responds to Arian claims, based on some biblical verses that speak of the Son as a created being, that the Son is not fully divine. The focus is on terms like "made" and "created," which seem to run counter to the notion of the Son's divinity. As we noted, Athanasius asserts that Scripture refers to the

49. *C. Ar.* 2.8.
50. *Ep. fest.* 45.

divinity in absolute terms without added qualification. Thus, "I and the Father are one," "I am the Truth," and "I am the Light of the world" are absolute statements about the Son without any qualifications or purpose. But when the Son takes flesh, he is assigned a cause, for "I came down from heaven, not to do my will, but the will of him that sent me."[51] For our sakes, he became incarnate, died on the cross, destroyed death by his resurrection, and gave us the renewal of life. There could be no resurrection without death, no death without a mortal body, no body without the incarnation. This is the reason for the incarnation. For "God did not send the Son into the world to condemn the world, but in order that the world might be saved through him."[52] The Son came into the world to heal the blind, raise the dead, and to save humanity; he came for our sake. Consequently, if he was created in the flesh, not for himself but for our sake, then he is not himself a creature, but he uses this language for us. As written in Ephesians, he has broken the wall of enmity, "in his flesh he has made both groups into one and has broken down the dividing wall, that is, the hostility between us. He has abolished the law with its commandments and ordinances, that he might create in himself one new humanity in place of the two, thus making peace."[53] The idea of "creating" a new humanity in himself so that we become renewed makes the language of Proverbs, "The Lord created me," suitable for him though he is not himself a creature.[54] This example of theological interpretation makes use of many of the methods outlined earlier. Athanasius has a clear *skopos* regarding the undisputed divinity of the Son, and he applies the principle that divinity is always

---

51. John 10:30; 14:6; 8:12; 6:38; *C. Ar.* 2.54.
52. John 3:17.
53. Eph 2:14–15.
54. *C. Ar.* 2.55.

articulated in absolute terms. In addition, he uses Scripture to interpret Scripture: his main argument is based on the Johannine texts but Ephesians clarifies and further affirms the theological premise of the divinity of the Son and that the language of "created" is only used after the incarnation.

Athanasius argues the interpretation of Isaiah 7:14, that a Virgin shall bear a son who shall be named Emmanuel, cannot be other than that God has come in the flesh. Peter taught Christ suffered for us in the flesh, for how could he suffer if he had not taken flesh?[55] He gave himself for us, he has undergone death in the flesh so that he might bring the power of death to naught. Thus, when we give thanks to Jesus Christ who came in the flesh to save us, we do not worship a creature but the Creator who has put on a created body for our salvation.[56] The Arians approve of the Jews worshiping God in the temple but do not approve of the worship of the Lord who is in the flesh as in a temple. The temple was a shadow created of stone and gold but when reality came the type ceased and the temple was destroyed. Thus, we worship the body of the Lord that was formed by the Holy Spirit and clothed the Word. Athanasius elaborates on the power of the flesh that clothed the Word and demonstrates that it was the Word's very own. It was the bodily hand that lifted Simon's mother-in-law and healed her from the fever.[57] It was Christ's human voice that spoke at the tomb of Lazarus and raised him from the dead.[58] It was the human hand stretched out on the cross that overcame death.[59] Athanasius explains that the created flesh formed by the Holy Spirit, because it is the Word's own, can

55. 1 Pet 4:1.
56. *Ep. Adelph.* 6.
57. Mark 1:31.
58. John 11:43.
59. *Ep. Adelph.* 7.

heal, raise the dead, and suffer on the cross for our salvation and thus is worthy of worship because it is God's own and in it we are worshiping God himself. This very specific notion that the humanity and the divinity perform the same act as one is the theological foundation of the concept of *monoenergeia*, a theological concept that unites the divinity and humanity in oneness and has theological and historical ramifications that will be discussed in a later chapter. In this example, Athanasius discusses several theological issues that might seem unconnected, but eventually these points merge together to build the larger picture of the incarnation and the incarnate Son. Athanasius's theological interpretation moves fluidly from the Old Testament to the New as one unit in which we see the shadow and type fulfilled as he elaborates on the understanding of the incarnate Son's humanity and divinity. Athanasius's theology is based on the bible and he uses this method of theological biblical interpretation to expound his theology. In the chapter on the Trinity there will be more illustrations of Athanasius's method of theological interpretation. This very short exposition is to alert the reader to Athanasius's method while discussing his theology.

SPIRITUAL INTERPRETATION

Athanasius believes Scripture strengthens the mind during spiritual warfare. The devil, according to Athanasius, envies humanity for having the blessings of knowing God through the words of Scripture. But the devil knows the human mind can be swayed to evil so he snatches away the seed of the Word sown within us. Christ sealed up his instructions in our hearts for us to treasure and warned us not to be led astray or deceived by the devil.[60] The Word bestowed on

60. Luke 21:1.

us a great gift and we should treasure the Word within our hearts and not be deceived by appearances as the grace of Holy Spirit will help us in discernment.[61] Athanasius believes that by reading and keeping within the treasury of our hearts the words of Scripture, and with the grace of the Holy Spirit, we strengthen our minds against any deception by which the devil attempts to sway us from God.

The Word became flesh for our sake, so when Proverbs says, "He founded me," the text is referring to his created humanity, following Athanasius's interpretive method that when a cause is specified (for his works) it refers to the humanity.[62] So, he is "founded," according to his humanity, so that we, as precious stones built upon his foundation, become a temple of the Holy Spirit who dwells within us. Similarly, he is the vine and we are his branches; we, as branches, are like him according to his humanity but not according to his divine essence. For the text does not say "he made me a foundation," lest the reader thinks he is a creation, but he "founded me." But for the sake of the stones he became a foundation taking what belongs to us, our humanity, so that through the likeness of the flesh, we may attain perfection and abide in immortality and incorruption.[63] Athanasius dwells at great length on Proverbs 8:22, interpreting it in various ways. In this instance he looks at it from a theological and spiritual perspective. He affirms the Son as "uncreated," but uses the verse to speak about the dwelling of the Holy Spirit within humanity. The incarnate Son is the foundation and vine that nourishes us to perfection. Taking what belongs to us, that is humanity,

---

61. *Ep. Aeg. Lib.* 1.

62. Prov 8:22. The LXX translation is: "The Lord made me the beginning of his ways for his works." Athanasius intentionally chose "foundation" rather than "made" to fit his interpretation.

63. *C. Ar.* 2.74.

he granted us salvation, which is the overcoming of death, immortality, incorruption, and attaining perfection.

Festal Letter 4 is a good example of the use of typology for spiritual instruction. Just as the Passover was a commemoration of the death of Pharaoh and the delivery of the people of Israel, so now we do celebrate not a temporal feast but a heavenly and eternal feast because the devil is slain. We do not celebrate in shadow but we celebrate it in truth. We do not eat the flesh of a lamb and anoint the doorpost with blood, we eat the Word of the Father and the blood of the New Testament seals the lentils of our hearts. The Savior has given us the grace of life, for he said, I am the Life.[64] Now everything is filled with joy and gladness because death is brought to naught and the whole world now knows the Lord. We should rid ourselves of the filthy garments and clothe our minds with pure garments. We observe that when Athanasius moves to the spiritual level, the focus shifts to the inner person represented in the mind, and the mind lifts the person to the heavenly realm. When we love virtue we are clothed with God, we exercise temperance, righteousness, humility, and have the strength of mind to not forget the poor.[65] Israel celebrated the Passover and victory in figure, but now the shadow is fulfilled and the type is accomplished, so let us go beyond the type and sing a new song.[66] We do not celebrate the Passover in Jerusalem, but celebrate it everywhere in the world. For in every place there is praise and worship to God since the gospel has spread to every place. Christ changed the type into the spiritual, for he did not eat with the disciples the flesh of the lamb but his own flesh, saying, take, eat and drink, this

64. John 14:6.
65. *Ep. fest.* 4:2, 3.
66. *Ep. fest.* 4:4.

is my body and my blood.[67] Athanasius took the Passover event as a shadow of old. The death of Pharaoh delivering Israel is a type fulfilled in Christ dying on the cross, overcoming death and saving humanity. The slain lamb is a type of the spiritual food of the body and blood of the Lord.

Athanasius's methods of interpretation are complex as he interweaves them in long expositions. He starts with one verse, but he uses so many other verses and various methods of interpretation to clarify its meaning that the reader may find it difficult to follow the intricacies of his thought. But following his thought in the interpretative process is rewarding and provides the reader with many insights into each verse he introduces.

In summary, Athanasius's interpretation is both theological and spiritual. Interpreting Scripture theologically became characteristic of Athanasius and of his successor Cyril of Alexandria, who elaborated and developed the method even further. Athanasius looks at the Old and New Testaments as one revelation in which the Old is a shadow and type of what is revealed and fulfilled in the New. He interprets verses within their context and within the *skopos* of the church's faith and tradition. Athanasius understood tradition as what Christ revealed in Scripture, what the apostles and their successors and teachers of the church taught, and what has been confirmed by the Council of Nicaea. The agreement of church leaders in Nicaea set a precedent that Athanasius considered authoritative, and the whole church would follow him; interpreting Scripture according to the *skopos* of the faith set in Nicaea and the later Councils became a guiding principle. Scripture is so important to Athanasius that he effortlessly weaves biblical verses and imagery into his writings; Scripture molds his theological language. Athanasius had such an extraordinary grasp of

67. *Ep. fest.* 4:4.

the entire biblical narrative, down to the minutest detail, that few modern scholars, even with the help of technology, can match it. Such mastery of the bible enabled him to interpret verses within their context and within the larger context of Scripture. Athanasius's close reading of Scripture enabled him to observe that Scripture refers to the divinity in absolute terms without qualifications of reason or cause. This principle is applied to both the Son and the Holy Spirit. Athanasius's method of the double accounts exposed the theological pitfalls into which the Arians fell and which led to great upheaval in the church. It should be noted that this method, though it clarified many interpretive difficulties the church faced during the Arian controversy, would not be emphasized by later theologians and the language of the "created body" or "created flesh" will disappear from the theological expressions of succeeding Alexandrian theologians. Athanasius uses the language of the created body to address the Arian concerns but at the same time he emphasizes that the created body was not that of a created being but of the Son of God. He augments the language of double accounts with the concept of the oneness of the *energia* to remove any division within the person of Christ. In general, Athanasius's theological interpretation had an impact on theology and set a trajectory for biblical interpretation in the Alexandrian Church.

QUESTIONS FOR FURTHER DISCUSSION

- What are the main methods Athanasius used in his biblical interpretation?
- What is the principle of the "double accounts" interpretation? Can you provide further examples of the "double accounts" principle from the gospels?

- Explain Athanasius's method of theological interpretation.
- Explain Athanasius's method of spiritual interpretation.

SUGGESTIONS FOR FURTHER READING

Festal Letter 1, 4, 6, 7, 14, 39
Orations against the Arians: 2:44–56; 3:18–29

4

THE TRINITY

ATHANASIUS DID NOT WRITE a comprehensive or systematic treatise to discuss the nature of God or the nature of the incarnate Son. His theology is in response to the heresies of his times and should be understood within this context. His theological masterpiece, *Against the Pagans-On The Incarnation*, which can be considered a full treatise on a subject, discusses the incarnation with few details about the nature of the Trinity. Most of his understanding of the Trinity is gleaned from his *Orations against the Arians*, his *Letters to Serapion concerning the Holy Spirit*, and a few other letters in response to specific concerns. Thus, polemical writings shape our knowledge of Athanasius's understanding of the Trinity, which explains why certain topics are not addressed. This chapter briefly introduces some of the heresies that were of concern to Athanasius and mentioned in his treatises or correspondence before discussing his views of the Trinity. Discussion of the divinity of the Son constitutes the major part of this chapter because the Arian controversy, which consumed theological thought during the fourth century, revolved around the divinity of the Son, both before and after the incarnation. The Holy Spirit will be discussed within the context of the polemics surrounding the Spirit's divinity.

HERESIES

Athanasius frequently mentions names of leaders of various heretical tendencies in his polemical writings: Arius, Eusebius of Nicomedia and the Eusebians, Asterius the Sophist, Eunomius, who took over from Aetius, Militius, Manichæus, Valentinus, Marcion, Basilides, Paul of Samosata, and the Tropikoi.[1] The following is a very short introduction to the main theological position of major names Athanasius mentions in his arguments. The aim is to acquaint the reader broadly with the larger context of the theological debates; Athanasius was contending not only with the Arians but with a larger spectrum of theological errors. Understanding the theological context of Athanasius's polemical writings will clarify Athanasius's emphasis on certain terms and themes.

Arius is the primary and most well-known antagonist in the historical debates of the fourth century. Arius was born in Libya and ordained a presbyter in the church of Baucalis in Alexandria during the tenure of Pope Alexander of Alexandria. He acquired some fame in Alexandria, initially because he was a persuasive speaker and later because of his controversial teachings. Not much of his writings has survived except for fragments of letters, a *Letter to Alexander of Alexandria*, and some excerpts from the

---

1. *C. Ar.* 2.21, 24, 40, 41, 43; *Ep. Serap.* 1.1.2.

Thalia.² Arius's ideas did not die with him; rather, those who would be called the Eusebians, the followers of Eusebius of Nicomedia, carried his banner and developed his ideas further even during the time of Athanasius.³ Arius believed God was unbegotten/uncaused (*agen[n]ētos*) and the creator of all things. Arius argued that if we attribute to the Son the attributes of God the Father, we will have "two unbegottens" or two causes which would be closer to Manichaean dualism. If the Son is from the Father, then he came to existence after a time interval; thus, Arius concludes his famous dictum, "once he (the Son) was not." If the Son did not exist once, and he is from the Father, then he came into being like the rest of creation and he is a creature. According to Arius, the Son is above other creations since he was created to help God in the act of creation. In addition, since Scripture attributes human characteristics to Christ, then Christ is human and the Son is not divine. Scripture also uses the language of "created" and "made" to speak of wisdom, as in Proverbs 8:22, which Arius referred to the Son. Terms such as "created," "made," "unbegotten/begotten," will be critical throughout Athanasius's writings. According to both Alexander of Alexandria and Athanasius of Alexandria the problem is that Arius focuses on biblical verses that describe the humanity and the economy of Christ and disregards those that discuss the divinity of the incarnate Son.

Athanasius mentions Asterius the Sophist in his writings.⁴ Asterius was from Cappadocia, a supporter of Arius,

2. *Arius Letter to Alexander of Alexandria* in *Syn*.16; Thalia in *C. Ar.* 1.5–7 and *Syn*.15.

3. Because of the introductory nature of this text and keeping with its objective, the ideas of Arius, the Eusebians, and their later followers will often be mentioned under the name of Arius.

4. *Decr*.8. *C. Ar.* 2.24; and *Syn.* 18, 19.

and a friend of Eusebius. Athanasius describes him as the "sacrificer" because he offered sacrifices, thus renouncing the faith, during the time of persecution.[5] According to Athanasius, Asterius preached in churches in Syria that the Wisdom of God was the creator of Christ and the rest of creation. Asterius wrote that because "power of God" and "wisdom of God" were written without the definite article, they are distinct from and generative of Christ.[6] Romans 1:20 says, "ever since the creation of the world his eternal power and divine nature, invisible though they are, have been understood and seen through the things he has made," which Asterius interprets to refer to the Father. Asterius made a distinction between the wisdom and power integral to the divine essence and those given to created beings. God's eternal power and wisdom are one and the same and "without beginning and unbegotten" (*anarchon te kai agennēton*) but Christ is the Only-Begotten and the Firstborn. Asterius concludes that the Son is a creature as he is the first of things whose intellectual nature shines upon the intellectual world.[7] Asterius insists that the Son is a being created by God's will.[8] The Father alone created the Son, and then the Son assisted the Father in the creation of the rest of creation.[9]

Eunomius was born in Cappadocia in the beginning of the fourth century. He studied under Aetius in Alexandria and was ordained bishop of Cyzicus in 360. Eunomius

---

5. *Syn.* 18.

6. 1 Cor 1:24: "Χριστὸν θεοῦ δύναμιν καὶ θεοῦ σοφίαν." The Greek text does not have an article but is translated with an article in NRSV "Christ the power of God and the wisdom of God."

7. *Syn.* 18, 19.

8. *C. Ar.* 2.24.

9. *Decr.* 8. Athanasius cites Asterius' *Syntagmation*, the fragments of which have been collected by Vinzent, *Asterius von Kappadokien*.

The Trinity

taught that the Son is "unlike" (*anomios*) the Father, thus his teaching came to be known as Anomian, but sometimes his followers are simply called Eunomians. Eunomius also taught that God's activity is distinct from his essence.[10] The Nicene Creed asserts that the Son is and of the same essence (*homoousios*) as the Father. The term *homoousios* caused a great debate as it was not a biblical term. The Anomians objected to the idea that the Son is of the same essence as the Father. They taught that the Father is unbegotten in essence and thus the Son, the Only-begotten, is of a different essence than the Father. The Son came to be by the will of God. The Holy Spirit is a creature sent by the Son.

Melitius, bishop of Lycopolis in Egypt, was of the opinion that the church should not be lenient with the lapsed, which caused a schism in the Egyptian church. Pope Peter of Alexandria excommunicated Melitius when he ordained presbyters outside of his jurisdiction who were sympathetic with his opinion. The Council of Nicaea resolved the problem by reinstating Melitius as bishop of Lycopolis, but with restrictions. He was not to ordain any bishops or presbyters and the presbyters ordained during the schism were to be under the supervision of Pope Alexander of Alexandria. Though the initial schism did not involve theological differences, after the eruption of the Arian controversy and the succession of Athanasius as bishop of Alexandria, the Melitians formed an alliance with the Arians.

Manicheans have a dualistic worldview that explains the existence of evil as a constant battle between light and darkness. They do not believe in a creator God nor one active in creation. Manicheanism was widespread at the time of Athanasius in Egypt and around the known world, and it had a strong intellectual and literary presence. It definitely required a Christian response to its understanding

---

10. Eunomius, *Apol.* 22.

of creation and the Godhead. Athanasius also attacked Valentinus and Carpocrates: the former claimed that the Son and the angels are of the same nature and the latter that the angels were the creators of the world.[11] Later in the same treatise Athanasius accuses Valentinus, Marcion, and Basilides of promoting the idea that angels created the world.[12] Valentinus believed the Christ did not assume a real flesh, a notion that aligns more with Docetism.[13] Athanasius also opposes Valentinus's claim that the Son is created by the will of the Father and is a "work of good pleasure."[14] Paul of Samosata, a third-century bishop of Antioch, seemed to deny the divinity and the preexistence of the Son and is mentioned several times in Athanasius's lists of heresiarchs.

The Tropikoi might be translated as "Misinterpreters" as Athanasius refers to their fallacious interpretation or "mode of exegesis" (*tropos*). Athanasius refers to the Tropikoi as "Spirit-fighters."[15] The Tropikoi claimed that the Holy Spirit was a creature based on their interpretation of Amos 4:13, among other verses. Athanasius refutes their claims with a series of biblical interpretations to set their "misinterpretation" right. Athanasius wrote *Letters to Serapion concerning the Holy Spirit* to oppose their teaching.

Athanasius did not believe those who followed heretical assertions should be called Christians. Thus he mentions that the followers of Marcion are called Marcionites, not Christians. He provides a list of heresiarchs whose followers are named after them and not called Christians: The followers of the Gnostic Valentinus, Basilides, Manichaeus, Simon Magus, Novatus, and Melitius are called

11. *C. Ar.* 1.56 (5).
12. *C. Ar.* 2.21.
13. *C. Ar.* 2.70.
14. *C. Ar.* 3.66, 67.
15. Athanasius and Didymus, *Works on the Spirit*, 21.

Valentinians, Basilidians, Manicheans, Simonians, and Melitians.[16] Though Athanasius was preoccupied with the Arians, he was also very aware of the other theological tendencies, with their various nuances, which fed on and made alliances with one other. All had to be addressed in his writings.

THE TRINITY

Christian theologians of the fourth century had to sort out a lot of questions, refine the theological language, and respond to the challenges that faced them. Athanasius posed some pithy questions that represent the crux of the problem. The major question is "was he?" or "was he not?" "Was" the Son always with the Father? or "was he not" from the beginning and thus was there a time before he came into existence? His list of pithy questions follow the same pattern: "Always" or "before his birth"? "Eternal" or "from this and from then"? "True" son or "by adoption"? "From participation" or "a thought"? "Came into existence [*genētōn*]" or "united to the Father"? "Unlike [*anomoion*] the Father in essence" or "like and proper [*omoion kai idion*] to the Father"? "A creature [*ktisma*]" or "through whom creatures came into existence [*gegenēsthai*]"? "Is he the Father's word" or is there "another word beside him" through whom he came to be [*gegenēsthai*]"? Is there another "wisdom" or is he alone named "Wisdom and Word"? Is he a partaker (*metochon*) of this wisdom?[17] Such is the language used in Athanasius's writings; all questions refer to major topics relevant to the understanding of the Godhead. Throughout the theological endeavor of Athanasius, these were the topics that consumed the discussions: Is the Son preexistent?

16. *C. Ar.* 1.3; *Ep. Adelph.* 2.
17. *C. Ar.* 1.9.

If not, then the Son is a creature and not divine. Is the Son eternal? Is the Son of the same nature and essence as the Father? Is the Son born, unbegotten, or unoriginate? Is the Son the Word of God, Wisdom, and Radiance? Is the Holy Spirit divine? These are the main questions around which most of Athanasius's arguments revolve as he attempts to respond to them to clarify the Christian understanding of the Trinity and the Godhead. These will be the major themes addressed in this chapter.

Athanasius acknowledges the unsuitability of the human mind to comprehend the fullness of the divinity and the incarnation. Nonetheless, he believes it is possible to express what God is not.[18] This came to be called apophatic theology, that is, to speak about what cannot describe or be attributed to God and the Trinity. Thus, Athanasius writes it is possible to condemn heretical assertions of the Son by saying what he is not; thus the Son is not a creature or a created being.[19] Such assertions further Athanasius's argument for the divinity of the Son.

Athanasius asserts the Trinity is one God of one origin, three of the same essence but not three gods. Athanasius notes he is asserting the one origin of the Godhead in opposition to Marcion and Manichæus. The Son is not external to the Godhead and the Son and the Holy Spirit are not from nothing, that is, they are not created beings. Athanasius argues we do not speak of three origins but one, as the sun has one radiance and its light is one, so the Trinity is one and not three gods. If the Son is external and the Holy Spirit is a creature, then we would be polytheists. Christians believe in one God through the Trinity and accordingly differ from the heretics who divide the Godhead into parts

18. *Ep. mon.* 1.2.
19. *Ep. mon.* 1.2.

The Trinity

of different kinds.[20] The origin, source, and essence of the three persons of the Trinity define the relationship of oneness of the three persons within the one Godhead.

Athanasius is Trinitarian in theology. His defense of the Son is for the sake of the Father and the Holy Spirit. Though most of the Arian controversy involved the nature of the Son, the necessity of defending the divinity of the Son involved defense of the Trinity. Our understanding of the Trinity entails speaking the truth about both the Son and the Holy Spirit. The truth about the Father cannot deny the Son who reveals the Father; similarly, we cannot deny the Son without denying the Holy Spirit.[21] If the Son and his divinity are denied, our understanding of the incarnation and the resurrection, the core of the Christian faith, will be in jeopardy. Athanasius argues that if God the creator, who creates through the Son, is not eternal and the Son, God's Word and Wisdom, is not eternal, then God is not the creator and the Son is external to the Godhead and not of the essence of the Father. If the Son and the Father are not both eternal, then the Trinity is not eternal. Against those who oppose the Trinity and call for a Monad and explain that the Son and the Holy Spirit were added to the Monad later, he argues that the Trinity would have been deficient before the Son and the Holy Spirit, being completed only after the creation of the Son and the Holy Spirit. The Trinity would thus be composed of natures and essences alien to each other. The Trinity would have a created consistency and we would worship a created being.[22] For Athanasius, Christian faith recognizes an unalterable and perfect Holy Trinity. If any person of the Trinity were to be created or a later addition, the divine essence of the Trinity would be

20. *C. Ar.* 3.15.
21. *C. Ar.* 1.8.
22. *C. Ar.* 1.17.

jeopardized and we would be left with a less-than-divine entity and a created God. The Trinity is indivisible and does not admit any addition or subtraction, for worship is to the indivisible Trinity.[23] There is one glory to the Holy Trinity. The nature of the Trinity is undivided and divine: to claim that the Father is eternal but the Son is not dishonors both Son and Father.

If the Father is divine and the Son a created being, then the Trinity is compound and the Holy Spirit would also rank with created entities. The essence of the divine is simple. Adding external or foreign elements transforms the simple divine nature to a compound, created nature. The Trinity ceases to have a divine essence. Athanasius concludes this inevitably divides and dissolves the Trinity. Athanasius further explains the indivisibility of the Trinity, saying that "the Spirit proceeds from the Father and, being proper to the Son, is given by him to the disciples and to all who believe in him."[24] Athanasius adds: "Seeing that there is such an order and unity in the Holy Trinity, who could separate either the Son from the Father, or the Spirit from the Son or from the Father himself?"[25] The Trinity is not compound and is indivisible. This assures the oneness of the nature and essence of the Trinity, its oneness of activity, and the oneness of worship.

An important aspect of Athanasius Trinitarian theology is the oneness of the activity (*energeia*) of the Trinity. He asks, "If the Father creates and renews all things through the Word in the Holy Spirit, what sort of likeness of kinship could the Creator have with creatures?"[26] The divine activity of creation and renewal is a Trinitarian activity,

23. *C. Ar.* 1.18.
24. *Ep. Serap.* 1.2.4.
25. *Ep. Serap.* 1.20.1.
26. *Ep. Serap.* 1.24.6.

which assures the indivisibility of the persons, who are all of the same nature. The Trinity is not divided into created and uncreated substances, which assures the oneness of the Trinity. "The gifts which the Spirit distributes to each are bestowed by the Father through the Word. For all that the Father has is the Son's. Thus what is given by the Son in the Spirit is a gift of the Father."[27] Whether it is the activity of creation, renewal, or the distribution of gifts, every activity is *from* the Father *through* the Son *in* the Holy Spirit. This oneness of activity preserves the understanding that the Trinity is one, undivided, of one nature and essence.

Athanasius gives a good summary of his understanding the Trinity in the following passage:

> For the holy and blessed Trinity is indivisible and united in itself. When the Father is mentioned, with him are both his Word and the Spirit who is in the Son. If the Son is named, the Father is in the Son, and the Spirit is not external to the Word. For there is one grace from the Father which is perfected through the Son in the Holy Spirit. And there is one divinity, and one God who is *over all, and through all, and in all.*[28]

GOD

Athanasius writes that the Trinity has not come into existence (*genētē*), there is one Godhead that is eternal, and the Holy Trinity has one glory and cannot be divided into different natures.[29] Though for the sake of discussion the Trinity is treated under a different title than God, theologically, the indivisibility of the Trinity has to be kept in

27. *Ep. Serap.* 1.30.5.
28. *Ep. Serap.* 1.14.6; words in italics are a citation of Eph 4:6.
29. *C. Ar.* 1.18.

mind. The same applies to each person of the Trinity, as Athanasius's defense of the Son as well as the Holy Spirit is for the sake of preserving the oneness and indivisibility of the Trinity and the Godhead.

Athanasius illustrates by an example from nature the indivisibility of the Godhead: when the sun shines, the radiance illuminates and the light cannot be detached as it is one and indivisible. Where the Father is, so is the Son. The oneness of the indivisible God is demonstrated in baptism. Athanasius writes the Father is one and the Son is one and the Son baptizes whomever the Father baptizes; and whomever the Son baptizes is perfected in the Holy Spirit.[30] We are baptized through and in the name of each person of the Trinity indivisibly. God is indivisible, and when the Arians introduce a Son that is created, they are describing two Gods, one that is unoriginate (*agenētō*) and the other that has an origin (*genētō*); they deny that the Son shares the same essence, nature and activities (*energeias*) of the Father.[31] If God is divisible we are not baptized in the name of the Trinity.

God is not only indivisible; he is also uncompounded, that is, not composite. The Arians and Asterius claim that the Son is not truly Son but he is called Word and Wisdom only in name. The true Wisdom of the Father coexisted with him without being generated, and this Wisdom made or created the Son. In this argument, the Arians allowed the Son to be called Son only in name. Athanasius refutes this proposal as it makes the Word and Wisdom complementary to the essence of God and creates a composite God. God is not composite, and the Son is truly Son.[32] God, the creator of all things, who compounded things into being, is

30. *C. Ar.* 2.41.
31. *C. Ar.* 3.16.
32. *C. Ar.* 2.38.

The Trinity

not composite. The nature of created, compounded entities differs from the nature of God their creator. God created things through the Word, so the essence of both God and the Word is not composite. The Word is Son in truth and is of the same essence as God.[33]

The Arians reasoned that Christ's increase in wisdom and suffering on the cross demonstrate that he is a created being for God does not increase in wisdom and does not suffer. Athanasius responds that it was the humanity that increased in wisdom and suffered, but the Son made the flesh his own and thus the suffering became God's own. The Arians used Luke 2:52 and similar verses in which Scripture says Jesus increased in wisdom, to claim that the Son is a created being. Athanasius expands such references to include Jesus' suffering in the flesh, hungering in the flesh, and being fatigued in the flesh to show that it was the flesh that increased in wisdom. But to say that the flesh increased in wisdom is to say that God increased in wisdom because the body was his own. The same can be said about his death.[34] For though God is impassible, he is passible in the flesh because he has taken a passible body. Such descriptions are attributed to the Son after the Word became flesh, for the hunger and fatigue are characteristic of the flesh, as are the increase in wisdom, suffering, and death. The body is God's body, it is his own. The increase in wisdom does not affect the Father's Light, which is the Son, but proves that the Word became flesh and that flesh is true flesh.[35] The flesh, that is, the humanity, increased in wisdom.[36] It

33. *Ep. Afr.* 8.

34. *C. Ar.* 3.54.

35. The insistence on the flesh being "true" is in opposition to the Marcionites and Manicheans who believed it "appeared" to be flesh, a type of Docetism.

36. *C. Ar.* 3.53 and *C. Ar.* 3.42–52.

was in this same flesh that he raised Lazarus from the dead, made the water wine, and healed the blind. Athanasius is advancing the case that, since the Arians recognized the humanity of Christ, they should also acknowledge the divinity manifested in the same body that suffered and increased in wisdom. The Arians misinterpret Scripture and undo the oneness (*enotēta*) of the Godhead, the oneness of Father and the Son, for "the Father and I are one."[37] Cyril of Alexandria, a successor of Athanasius, emphasizes the oneness of the person of Christ, not only of the Godhead. It is necessary to affirm that the incorporeal took a mortal and corruptible body so that the things proper to the flesh, such as suffering and hunger, are attributed to God as well as to the body.[38] Athanasius affirms everything that is attributed to the humanity is true, otherwise the incarnation is only in appearance, God is divisible, and composite. If the Son had not become flesh, and this flesh were not true flesh, then God, to whom is attributed everything that is attributed to the flesh, would not have suffered on the cross, overcome death, and renewed humanity. This also demonstrates that the Son is of the same essence as the Father as well as the oneness of the activity of the Godhead.

THE FATHER

Athanasius argues that calling God Father surpasses calling him unoriginate. The title "unoriginate" (*agenētos*) is relative to all the works that are "originate," that is, came into being through the Word, but the title "Father" is relative only to the Son. And the title "Father" is scriptural: "Do you not believe that I am in the Father and the Father is in me? The words that I say to you I do not speak on my own;

37. John 10:30; *C. Ar.* 3.55.
38. *C. Ar.* 3.56.

The Trinity

but the Father who dwells in me does his works. Believe me that I am in the Father and the Father is in me"; and "The Father and I are one."[39] Scripture does not call the Father unoriginate and we are not baptized in the name of the unoriginate, but we are baptized in the name of the Father, Son, and Holy Spirit. However, through baptism, we, created beings who are originate, become sons.[40]

Athanasius lists the attributes of the Father as follows: "The Father is eternal, immortal, powerful, light, King, Sovereign, God, Lord, Creator [*ktistēs*], and Maker [*poiētēs*]."[41] Because Athanasius's focus is on showing the divinity of the Son, we often must extract his understanding of the Father from his arguments about the Son. For example, God is Reason (*Logos*).[42] There was no time when the Father was without Reason, for reason is part of the Father's own (*idion*) essence. To add Reason to God would be to change God, who is unchangeable. In the same way, God is Light and the Father's radiance is part of his essence. No one inquires into the radiance of the sun; otherwise, the light and radiance would be external to the sun, which is not the case. Radiance is part of the sun's own (*idion*) essence. We cannot say that there was a time when the sun was without radiance or radiance was not part of the essence of light. The Son is the radiance of God's glory, so we cannot consider the Word as an addition to the Father and external to the Father, for the Son is begotten of the Father.[43] The Son was

39. John 14:10,11; and 10:30.
40. *C. Ar.* 1.34.
41. *C. Ar.* 1.21.
42. *C. Ar.* 1.24, 25.
43. *C. Ar.* 1.25; *C. Ar.* 2.33. Heb 1:3 is critical for this interpretation as it speaks of the Son as being a radiance of God's glory and an impress of his very being, and upholding all things by the word of his power.

always with the Father, not external to the Father or a later addition to the Father. The Son was always with the Father and then became flesh. As radiance is proper to the light and all things of the light are of the radiance, so is the Son in relation to God.[44] The Father is the source of all grace and peace, and when the Father gives these gifts, the Son gives it for "in the Image is contemplated the Father, and in the Radiance is the Light."[45] There are not two sources of grace or gifts, all gifts are from the Father through the Son and in the Holy Spirit.

God the Father always had the power to make, and all creation is made through the Son.[46] All created things that came into existence are external to the creator and do not have the power to be eternal. The Son is the eternal offspring of the Father and is the Father's own and of his essence.[47] Athanasius adds another dimension to his argument: if the Son is a created being and is created for the sake of bringing things into being, this detracts from the Father who thus appears incapable of creation and in need of assistance.[48] Arius also claimed that the Son was merely an instrument (*organon*) used by the Father for creation, which Athanasius opposed as making the Son external to the Father and a created being, not of the essence of the Father.[49]

The title "Father" is significant. The essence of the Son is the same as that of the Father. The Son is the Image of the Father. The Image must have these attributes to make it true

44. *C. Ar.* 3.36.
45. *C. Ar.* 3.11.
46. John 1:3.
47. *C. Ar.* 1.29.
48. *C. Ar.* 2.25.

49. Athanasius also does not consider the body of Christ as an instrument. Farag, "*Organon*," 93–105.

that whoever has seen the Son, has seen the Father.[50] Therefore, the Son has to have all the attributes of the Father or he would not be the Image of the Father and of the essence of the Father. The Father does not change and consequently the Image does not change. Therefore, if change is attributed to the Son, then change is attributed to the Father who does not change.[51] To understand the Father, we listen to what the Son reveals about himself and about the Father. If we diminish the Son, we diminish the Father. If the Arians claim that the Son is a created being, then they detract from the essence of the Father and add change to the essence of the unchangeable God. The Father and the Son are at the core of our understanding of the Trinity and any attempt by the Arians to undermine the Son for the sake of the Father undermines the Trinity.

THE SON

Athanasius writes: "God has a Son, the Word, the Wisdom, the Power, that is, His Image and Radiance; from which it at once follows that He is always; that he is from the Father; that He is like; that He is the eternal offspring of His essence; and there is no idea involved in these of creature [*ktismatos*] or work [*poiēmatos*]."[52] The themes and terms for the Son's attributes in this quotation were rallying cries used by the Arians against the divinity of the Son and taken over and defended by Athanasius in his refutation of the Arians. Whether the Son is divine or a created being is at the core of the Arian controversy.

Athanasius took several approaches to defend the Son's divinity. One of these approaches is to correct Arian

50. John 14:9; *C. Ar.* 1.21.
51. *C. Ar.* 1.22.
52. *C. Ar.* 2.34.

misinterpretations of biblical verses that use terms such as "created" or "made." Athanasius asserts that they refer to the humanity of the incarnate Son. Athanasius explains that when John says that the Word became flesh, it should not be understood that the whole Word was transformed and became flesh, but that he put on flesh and became man. When Proverbs says that the Lord "created [*ektisen*] me,"[53] it should not be understood that the whole Word became a creature (*ktisma*) in nature but that the Word put on a created body. It is through this created body taken by Christ as his own that we are renewed (*anakainisthēnai*) and made divine (*theopoiēthēnai*).[54] Athanasius clarifies that the Word took what belongs to humanity, everything that belongs to its created nature, as his own to renew the fallen humanity. The incarnation did not change anything of the divine nature but its purpose was to renew human nature and make it divine (*theopoiēthēnai*). This renewal cannot take place unless the divinity empties itself, without any change of its nature, to raise humanity up to its former status as image of God. Athanasius is very careful to call the body "created" but not to ascribe createdness to the whole of the incarnate Word so as not to give the attribute "created" to the Word itself. Verses that ascribe human attributes to the incarnate Son Arians interpreted as referring to the Son before the incarnation. Thus Athanasius emphasizes the "created body" to counter any notion of createdness attributed to the totality of the incarnate Son, or to the Son before the incarnation, and to restrict createdness entirely to the body, which represents the fullness of humanity at the time of the incarnation.

The emphasis on the body as created was forced on Athanasius by the Arian controversy and explains the

53. Prov 8:22.
54. *C. Ar.* 2.47.

The Trinity

double-accounts approach to scriptural interpretation. The use of double accounts in theological discourse was abandoned after the settlement of the Arian controversy, after which the idea that he took a body "as his own" was emphasized. In addition, to eliminate separation or division within the person of Christ the "created" body language was supplemented with the idea of the oneness of the activity of the person of Christ. The principle of *communication idiomatum*, the exchange of idioms or properties, which emerged centuries later, cannot be applied here. According to that principle the properties of each nature of the incarnate Son can be exchanged. If the *communicatio idiomatum* were applied in this case then the createdness of the flesh of the incarnate Son would be applied to the divinity so that the divinity would be created and the Son a creature, which is exactly what Athanasius was opposing. Athanasius discusses and defends the divine essence, not the properties of the incarnate Son.

Athanasius's close reading of Scripture, paying special attention to the use of terms, was another means he used to defend the divinity of the Son. Athanasius emphasizes throughout his writings that what is labeled "created" or "made" is only relevant to creatures and cannot be attributed of the divinity and accordingly not to any person of the Trinity. Genesis 1:1 says, "God created heaven and earth." Psalm 119:73 says, "Your hands have made and fashioned me"; it does not say, "You have begotten me."[55]

---

55. It should be noted that Genesis 1 uses two words to describe the activity of creation. For example, in Genesis 1:1, 21, and 27 the Hebrew word בָּרָא (*bara'*) is used for "to create" and in Genesis 1:7, 16, 25, 27, and 31 the Hebrew word עָשָׂה (*'ashah*) is used for "to make." In the LXX both words are translated in Greek as *poieō*, "to make." Since Athanasius is a LXX reader and user, "to make" became representative of all acts of creation and is always used when speaking about creatures or creation.

The verb "made" is always used with creatures but when speaking about the Son it is always "beget." What is made always has a beginning, that is, it is "originate" (*genētos*), but God has no beginning because he was not made and is therefore "unoriginate" (*agenētos*). The Word of God also did not have a beginning and was always with the Father. Since all things came to be through the Word, it is evident that the Word was before the beginning of creation.[56] All originate things came to be through the Word. When Scripture speaks about Job, Moses, or Abraham as begetting sons, it speaks about human generation. Scripture is clear that while what is generated may be spoken of using "become" or "made," originate things (*genēta*) cannot be called generate (*gennēta*), that is, begotten.[57] Athanasius is careful to point out that comparison implies oneness of kind; we cannot compare the Son with originate things because we are comparing things of different kind and essence.[58] For example, we cannot compare the essence of the Son with angels because the angels are originate while the Son is not.[59] God is beyond comparison and cannot be compared to humanity, which is also originate.[60] The term "become" when used of the Son indicates the Son's ministry and the economy, not his essence.[61] It also refers to his incarnate presence as he bore our sins in his own body on the cross.[62] Athanasius flags terms that when used should be understood

56. *C. Ar.* 2.57.
57. *C. Ar.* 1.56.
58. *C. Ar.* 1.58.
59. *C. Ar.* 1.56 (5). Athanasius is responding to Valentinus, Carpocrates, and other heretics who believed that Christ was one with the Angels.
60. *C. Ar.* 1.57; *C. Ar.* 1.59 (7).
61. *C. Ar.* 1.62.
62. *C. Ar.* 1.62 (12).

either about creatures, the humanity of the incarnate Son, or the Son's ministry and economy among us.

Athanasius takes the terms "created" and "made" further. He says that Scripture differentiates between the Offspring (*gennēma*, "begotten one") and creation. Creation is not of the essence of God but external to him. The Son is described as an Offspring and eternal, but when referring to things made, Scripture indicates that they came to be, they had a beginning, they are external works of the maker. John writes, "In the beginning was the Word," not "in the beginning the Word has become," or "been made," but "was," for the Word always and eternally existed; the Son is the begotten of the Father.[63] We are God's creation and later we were made sons, but the Son is Son by nature and from the beginning. The Word who is in us who gave us the right to cry "Abba, Father" made us sons of God, but we are not sons by nature.[64]

While clarifying the significance of the terms "created" and "made," Athanasius gives a concise explanation of the difference between "created" and "begotten." God, who is the Father of the Word by nature, the begotten Word, becomes creator and maker of the flesh that the Word takes on when he becomes flesh. On the other hand, God the creator becomes the father of humanity because the Word was dwelling in humanity. When humanity received the Spirit of the Son, we became children of God. When the Word put on a created nature and became like us, he was called the Firstborn for our sake. When the Son for our sake raised his own body, for the flesh, being the Word's body, was the first to be free and is the first to rise, he becomes the Firstborn from the dead for he abolished death. Because he rose from the dead, we also rise in due course from the dead. The flesh

63. *C. Ar.* 2.58.
64. *C. Ar.* 2.59; *C. Ar.* 3.25.

that rose from the dead for our sake is created for the sake of the economy and for the sake of our salvation, but the Son was begotten and is Word by nature.[65] When he rose from the dead, he healed our wounds and perfected us and renewed us. When he overcame death we no longer fear death but will be forever with Christ in the heavens.[66]

Athanasius also defends the divinity of the Son when he discusses the divine attributes of the Father, asserting that they are also attributes of the Son. The Son is eternal as the Father is eternal. The Son never said, "I became Truth" but "I am the Truth." "I am" signifies eternity.[67] Athanasius asserts that any addition or change to the Father demonstrates an imperfect Godhead. For if the Son was created after the Father, then the essence of the Father was imperfect until the Son was added; but he is of God's own essence who is everlasting and eternal.[68] Athanasius asserts that these attributes belong to the Son: the Son is eternal and not created, he is of the essence of the Father, and there was no time interval separating the Son from the Father.

That the essence of the Son is the same as the essence of the Father was made clear when the voice from heaven proclaimed, "This is my beloved Son."[69] The Son is of the essence of the Father; he is eternal, not external or an addition to the Father as he is not created; he is the Truth, Image, Radiance, and Word of the Father. Athanasius devotes special attention to the attribute of Radiance. The metaphor of the sun and its radiance is a helpful theological argument for refuting claims that the Son is a created being and, especially, that the Son is separated from the Father in time. The

65. *C. Ar.* 2.61.
66. *C. Ar.* 2.67.
67. *C. Ar.* 1.12.
68. *C. Ar.* 1.14.
69. Matt 3:17.

The Trinity

Son's being the Radiance of God assumes the eternity of the Son and directly opposes the Arian rallying cry that the Son was not always with the Father. Athanasius uses Hebrews 1:3, which speaks about the Son being the radiance of God's glory and the impress of his essence. There was no time when God was not with what is proper to him and what is proper to him and is his own belongs to his essence. God is eternal and his Radiance is eternal. Athanasius argues that, as the word is in the thought, and the sun in the radiance, and the stream in the fountain, whoever contemplates the Son contemplates the Father's own essence.[70] In all of these metaphors there is no time or thought interval. Athanasius again uses the metaphor from nature that "the radiance also is light, not second to the sun, nor different from light, nor from participation of it, but a whole and proper offspring of it."[71] Though the sun has one light and not two, the sun and radiance are two; similarly the Father and the Son are indivisible but two.[72] Because the Son is the offspring of the Father, the attributes and essence of the Father are the Son's own.[73] For the Son is in the Father and the Father is in the Son: "I and the Father are one" reveals the identity and the oneness of the essence and nature of the Godhead. The Father and the Son are inseparable.[74] Such metaphors clarify the language of the Nicene Creed. The theological discussion here highlights the intention of the Creed's use of such expressions as "light from light" to emphasize that there was no time interval between Father and Son: they are of the same essence and attributes, and the Son is not a created being. The Son is indivisible from the Father but still

70. *C. Ar.* 3.3.
71. *C. Ar.* 3.4.
72. *C. Ar.* 3.4.
73. *C. Ar.* 3.5.
74. *C. Ar.* 3.6.

distinct. It is a succinct metaphor that clarifies the complex theological doctrine of the Trinity.

God is unchangeable and his Image and Word is equally unchangeable. When the Word became flesh, the Word and his nature remained unchangeable.[75] When Philippians 2:5–11 describes Christ humbling himself and then being exalted, the humility is not a reward, nor is the exaltation, which simply indicates that he is equal to the Father and receives equal worship.[76] Because humility pertains to his humanity and the economy of salvation, and on account of the body that is his own, when he received exaltation, we were exalted with him. The Word did not receive exaltation for he possesses it according to his divinity.[77] For our sake and for our sanctification, he provides for humanity the exaltation and the indwelling of the Spirit within us. Similarly, when Christ says that "for their sakes I sanctify myself, so that they also may be sanctified in truth," Christ is the sanctifier, he is the Lord of sanctification. He sanctifies himself so that we are sanctified in truth.[78] Similarly, when he is baptized, we are baptized in him.[79] Athanasius provides all these examples of humility, of exaltation, of sanctification, and of baptism to explain that the Word did not need any of these "exaltations" and he did not receive them for his own sake, but it is humanity who received them through him. He does not need exaltation for he is unchangeable. God's Word is unchangeable.[80]

Athanasius discusses the incarnation to further dismantle the Arian claims. Athanasius stresses that the Son

75. *C. Ar.* 1.36, 37.
76. *C. Ar.* 1.40.
77. *C. Ar.* 1.44.
78. John 17:19–20; *C. Ar.* 1.46.
79. *C. Ar.* 1.48.
80. *C. Ar.* 1.49, 51, 52.

became human and did not come into a human being. The former describes the Word become flesh, the latter, the Lord's coming to the prophets or only appearing to people.[81] Athanasius emphasizes the Word becoming flesh and taking it as his own, without which our renewal and salvation cannot be complete. This understanding of the incarnation will have important repercussions in the following centuries, especially during the Nestorian controversy. If the Word appeared to people or indwelled a single human person, not taking the full humanity as his own to save, he would have saved only one person. Or if he was speaking through a person, as the Word did through the prophets, then there is no incarnation but a continuation of the revelations of the Old Testament. When the prophets suffered, Scripture never says that God suffered; however, when the Word became flesh and suffered on our behalf, Scripture says that he suffered for us in the flesh.[82]

Athanasius writes that the word "flesh" refers to the fullness of humanity, constituted of body, soul, and sense or intelligence.[83] Joel describes "my Spirit" poured on all flesh meaning human beings. Similarly, Daniel affirms that he worships the Living God who has sovereignty over all flesh. In both cases, Athanasius argues, by the term "flesh" Scripture refers to humanity.[84] If the flesh of the incarnate Son does not include the fullness of humanity—body, soul, and intelligence/reason—if the flesh meant only the body, then the incarnate Son would have saved only part of the human person. Athanasius emphasizes, "became flesh" does not mean that the Word was transformed into flesh

81. *C. Ar.* 3.30.
82. 1 Pet 4:1; *C. Ar.* 3.31.
83. *Tom.* 7, 11.
84. *C. Ar.* 3.30; *Ep. Epict.* 7, 8; Joel 2:28; Bel 1:5 LXX.

and bones but that he became flesh in the full sense, and this flesh became his own.[85]

When the Word became flesh, the body became his own and the properties of the flesh are his own. Accordingly, the suffering of the flesh is God's suffering as are its hunger and thirst. At the same time, the Word heals the sick and raises the dead also through the body. "And the Word bore the infirmities of the flesh, as His own, for His was the flesh; and the flesh ministered to the works of the Godhead, because the Godhead was in it, for the body was God's."[86] Athanasius points out that Isaiah 53:4 says that he "carried," and not "remedied," our sins to indicate that he himself carries our sins and infirmities in his own body and not as an external activity. He became incarnate for our sake and in the body that is his, he carries our sins on the tree, that is the cross, for the sake of our salvation so that we are "filled with the righteousness of the Word."[87]

The theological proposition that when the body became the Word's own, the properties of the flesh also became his own is at the core of Athanasius's theological thinking. It is this concept that makes possible Athanasius's double-accounts interpretation without causing any division or duality within the person of Christ. Athanasius gives specific examples to illustrate his theological concept. Christ stretched his hands humanly to Peter's mother-in-law but he stopped the illness divinely. He used his human spittle mixed with clay and spread it on the eyes of the man born blind and divinely healed him. He gave forth a human voice through which he divinely raised Lazarus from the dead. Athanasius explains that these miracles were done with the clear participation of both the humanity and the divinity to

85. *Ep. Epict.* 7, 8.
86. *C. Ar.* 3.31.
87. *C. Ar.* 3.31.

assert that he has a true body and not only the appearance of a body, that the body is his own, and all that is proper to the body is proper to the Son.[88] Every activity involved both the humanity and the divinity working together in unity. The oneness of activity would not have taken place had the body not been his own but external to him.

It is through the divine activities that took place through the body that we are made divine. Had not the properties of the flesh been the Word's own humanity we would not have been set free.[89] Humanity remained mortal and corruptible from the time of Adam's transgression, but now that the Word has taken humanity as his own and appropriated everything to himself, death no longer has power over the flesh "and henceforth men no longer remain sinners and dead according to their proper affections, but having risen according to the Word's power, they abide ever immortal and incorruptible."[90] The Word transferred to himself everything that belongs to humanity and made it his own so that we, now proper to the Word, may share eternal life. We do not die according to our origin in Adam, "but henceforward our origin and all infirmity of flesh being transferred to the Word, we rise from the earth, the curse from sin being removed, because of Him who is in us, and who has become a curse for us, and with reason; for as we are all from earth and die in Adam, so being regenerated from above of water and Spirit, in the Christ we are all quickened; the flesh being no longer earthy, but being henceforth made Word, by reason of God's Word who for our sake 'became flesh.'"[91]

88. *C. Ar.* 3.32; *C. Ar.* 3.41.
89. *C. Ar.* 3.33.
90. *C. Ar.* 3.33.
91. *C. Ar.* 3.33.

The term *homoousion*, meaning "of the same essence," is used in the Nicene Creed but is hardly mentioned in Athanasius's writings. The term was the subject of a long controversy. There was a lot of objection to the term as it is not biblical and might be interpreted in Sabellian terms for not distinguishing sufficiently among the persons of the Trinity. Throughout Athanasius's treatises he insists that the Son is of the same essence as the Father, as we have discussed throughout this chapter, but he avoids using the term *homoousion*. But though he avoids the term in his writings, Athanasius strongly defends its use. In addition, he defended "of the *same* essence" rather than "like in essence."[92] Athanasius argues if the Son is not of the same essence as the Father, then he is a created being,[93] and the unity of the Godhead is lost.[94] Athanasius was hesitant to accept terms other than *homoousion*, and in the end *homoousion* remained in the Nicene Creed when it was revised at the Council of Constantinople to include the Holy Spirit. Throughout the Arian controversy, Athanasius defended the divinity of the Son, maintaining the Son is not created or made but is of the same essence as the Father. The Son has the same attributes as the Father. For he is eternal and unchangeable, being the Father's Image and Radiance. When the Son took the fullness of humanity none of his attributes were changed and he remained divine and of the same essence of the Godhead.

THE HOLY SPIRIT

Athanasius's theology on the Holy Spirit is gleaned from two main sources, both polemical: his *Orations against the*

92. *Syn.* 53.
93. *Syn.* 35.
94. *Syn.* 50.

Arians (AD 339–46) and his *Letters to Serapion concerning the Holy Spirit* (AD 358–59) responding to the Tropikoi. Athanasius had two main concerns: to defend the divinity of the Holy Spirit, and to establish the place of the Holy Spirit within the Trinity.

The Tropikoi taught that the Holy Spirit is a creature and that it has an angelic status; the former teaching is the same as that which the Arians used to describe the Son. As in the case of the Son, Athanasius's argument against the Tropikoi is that they misinterpreted Scripture. For example, the Tropikoi misinterpreted the passage in Amos 4:13, which according to Athanasius's text reads, "Therefore I am the one who gives strength to thunder and who creates spirit and who proclaims his Christ to humanity."[95] If God creates spirit, the Tropikoi concluded, then the spirit is a creature. Athanasius argued that the term "spirit" here refers to wind rather than the Holy Spirit as the Holy Spirit is never referred to without qualification.[96] In this verse, "spirit" is used without qualification, therefore it refers to "a spirit" or in this case "the wind."[97] Scripture uses "spirit" to refer to the spirit of a human being, or spirit as in Genesis, or divine Word, newness of spirit, referring to the spirit and not the letter, and other variant meanings.[98]

The Tropikoi also misinterpreted 1 Timothy 5:21, which according to Athanasius's text reads, "In the presence of God and Jesus Christ and the elect angels, I charge you to observe these things without prejudice, doing nothing out of partiality." The Tropikoi concluded that the "elect angels"

---

95. *Ep. Serap.* 1.3.1. It should be noted that the LXX uses the term "create/*ktizōn*" with spirit or wind.

96. *Ep. Serap.* 1.4.1. This was discussed in chapter 3 under "Methods of Interpretation." See pages 60–68.

97. *Ep. Serap.* 1.8.4—10.1. Modern translations use "wind."

98. *Ep. Serap.* 1.8.1.

refer to the Holy Spirit, as they are mentioned after God and Christ.[99] Athanasius explains that the angels, who are minsters to human affairs, were mentioned as "witness who observe what is said."[100] Athanasius's defense of the divinity of Holy Spirit is for the preservation of the Trinity, for if the Holy Spirit is a creature, then the Son must be a creature for the Spirit is in the Son and the Son is in the Father and if the Son or the Spirit is separated then we "destroy the perfection of the Trinity."[101] In the *Letters to Serapion concerning the Holy Spirit* Athanasius defends the divinity of the Holy Spirit. He lists ways Scripture describes the Holy Spirit: it is from God and it is the Spirit of sanctification and renewal.[102] The Spirit is life-giving.[103] The Spirit is an anointing and a seal.[104] Humanity partakes of God through the Spirit.[105]

Athanasius explains that all things partake of the Spirit and the Spirit takes from the Son.[106] Athanasius here extends the relationship of the Holy Spirit to the whole of creation in addition to the Trinity. All things that partake of the grace of the Spirit come from the Son, and as we partake of the Son, we partake of God.[107] All things partake of the Son who sanctifies all things in the Spirit.[108] The Psalm says the Son is anointed. He is anointed in the humanity that he has taken as his own with the oil of gladness, that is, the Holy Spirit, as is written in Isaiah 61:1, so that he

99. *Ep. Serap.* 1.10.4.
100. *Ep. Serap.* 1.14.7.
101. *Ep. Serap.* 1.21.1, 3.
102. *Ep. Serap.* 1.22.1, 3; Rom 1:4.
103. *Ep. Serap.* 1.23.2; Rom 8:11.
104. *Ep. Serap.* 1.23.4; 1 John 2:27.
105. *Ep. Serap.* 1.24.1; 1 Cor 3:16–17.
106. *C. Ar.* 1.15.
107. *C. Ar.* 1.16.
108. *C. Ar.* 1.46.

provides for humanity the indwelling of the Holy Spirit. His anointing provides not only exaltation and resurrection for humanity, it also provides the indwelling of and building up of friendship with the Holy Spirit.[109] It is not the indwelling spoken about of Aaron or David; it is Christ's receiving the Spirit for our sake so that what dwells in him dwells in us because the body is his own.[110] The Son is sanctified for our sake in his humanity so that when Scripture describes the descent of the Spirit on him in the Jordan, it is the descent of the Spirit upon humanity because the Son has taken human nature as his own. When he received the Spirit in the Jordan, it was humanity that received the Spirit. When he was baptized, it was humanity that was baptized in him. Because of us and for us he was anointed in the flesh he assumed so that the sanctification received by him in his humanity may come to all humanity from him.[111] Christ did not need to be anointed or sanctified, nor did this anointing alter his essence in any way; he was anointed for our sake so that through him humanity is sanctified. The Lord is the giver of the Spirit, the Father gives it through the Son, and it is given to us out of the Son's fullness. Therefore, he who blasphemes against the Spirit blasphemes against the Son, whose Spirit it is.[112]

The Spirit is God's gift to humanity that is given to us through the Son.[113] The incarnate Son called the Father Lord so that when we receive the Spirit through him, by the gift of the Spirit we call the Lord Father.[114] The Son is son by nature but we are by adoption through the Son in the

109. *C. Ar.* 1.46; Ps 45:7.
110. *C. Ar.* 1.47.
111. *C. Ar.* 1.47.
112. *C. Ar.* 1.50.
113. *C. Ar.* 2.18.
114. *C. Ar.* 2.51.

Spirit. This is the gift of adoption given to us through the incarnation of the Son, through whom in the Spirit we are able to call God "Abba, Father." Athanasius explains when Proverbs 3:19 says wisdom founded the earth, it does not mean the Son is a created being but refers to his humanity, which he took for our sake. We are the precious stones in the building of his humanity and we become the temple of the Holy Spirit that dwells in us. The Son is the foundation, we are the stones built upon him. He took humanity for our sakes, taking what is ours so that through him the Holy Spirit dwells within us and we attain perfection and abide in immortality and incorruptibility.[115]

The divinity of the Holy Spirit as one of the persons of the Trinity has been affirmed in the Nicene Creed.[116] In addition, in a few, though not all, of his writings, Athanasius ends with Trinitarian doxologies, as when he speaks of those who "love the God and Father, in Christ Jesus our Lord: through Whom and with Whom be to the Father Himself, with the Son Himself, in the Holy Spirit, honor and might and glory for ever and ever. Amen";[117] or of "all them that 'have loved the appearing' of our Lord, and Savior, and God, and universal King, Jesus Christ; through whom to the Father be glory and dominion in the Holy Spirit, both now and for ever, world without end, Amen."[118] These greetings indicate that doxologies to the Trinity in the form "to the Father, through the Son, in the Holy Spirit" were common practice at the time of Athanasius. The Trinity was at the center of Alexandrian thought.

---

115. *C. Ar.* 2.74.

116. As well as in many references in Athanasius's corpus such as *Tomus ad Antiochenos* and *Letters to Serapion concerning the Holy Spirit*.

117. *Inc.* 57.

118. *Ep. Aeg. Lib.* 23.

We have not presented all the dimensions of Athanasius's Trinitarian theology, nor have we even covered the full extent of the main points of his theology. We have instead highlighted the main themes Athanasius constantly emphasized, those relevant for his understanding of God and the Trinity, and those relevant to present-day Christians' understanding the roots of Christian theological thought. We also want to provide familiarity with the terms and vocabulary Athanasius uses in his writings, hoping it will encourage the reading of Athanasius's literary corpus. The language of Athanasius and the theological themes covered in this chapter clarify the language of the Nicene Creed. The summary of this chapter is the Nicene Creed; it encapsulates all that Athanasius spent his lifetime defending.[119]

QUESTIONS FOR FURTHER DISCUSSION

- What are the main theological themes addressed in the chapter on the Trinity? How does the Nicene Creed reflect this theolgoy?
- Athanasius defended the divinity of the Son; however, his theology is Trinitarian and not Christocentric. Explain.
- How did Athanasius explain the oneness of the Trinity and the oneness of the Son?
- What is Athanasius's contribution to the understanding of the Holy Spirit?

SUGGESTIONS FOR FURTHER READING

The Three *Orations against the Arians*

---

119. Appendix 2 has a comparative chart of the Nicene Creed and the Nicaean-Constantinopolitan Creed.

Letters to Serapion concerning the Holy Spirit (preferable the translation of DelGogliano and Radde-Gallwitz.)
Letter to Epictetus
Tome to the People of Antioch
On the Councils of Ariminum and Seleucia (especially sections 33–55)

5

ENERGEIA AND *THEOPOIĒSIS*

Activity and Making Divine

ATHANASIUS OF ALEXANDRIA is known for his orthodoxy and defense of the faith. He defended the divinity of the Son throughout his polemical writings. We have also seen his defense of the Trinity, his defense of the divinity of the Holy Spirit, his understanding of salvation, his understanding of evil and the human person. This chapter will discuss two important aspects of Athanasius's theology: *energeia* and *theopoiēsis*. Both theological concepts have been mentioned throughout our discussion and are part of the building blocks that formed Athanasius's orthodoxy. For Athanasius the concept *energeia* or "activity" cements the oneness of the Trinity. Two successors of Athanasius, Cyril of Alexandria and Timothy II of Alexandria, develop the concept on this Athanasian foundation. Athanasius encapsulates his understanding of salvation in his famous dictum: "For he became human that we might be made god (*theopoiēthōmen*)."[1] This should not be confused with *theōsis*, which is translated as "deification" and "divinization." *Theōsis* is a term coined by Gregory of Nazianzus and is distinctly different from Athanasius's *theopoiēsis*. These two concepts, *energeia* and *theopoiēsis*, have been taken up and had their theological mark on ancient as well as modern theologians. This chapter will look at these two concepts as Athanasius understood and used them.

ENERGEIA

The term *energeia* does not have an exact English equivalent and has different meanings in different contexts. In general, it can be translated as "activity or operation." It is sometimes translated as "action or energy."[2] Some translators use the term "work" or "action" to express the activity undertaken. This chapter will use the term "activity" or simply the transliterated Greek, *energeia*.[3] The term *energeia* refers to either the divine activity or the activity of the incarnate Son.[4] In this chapter we will discuss first the activity of the Trinity, then look briefly at human activity, and finally discuss the activity of the incarnate Son.

---

1. *Inc.* 54.

2. See Liddell et al., *Greek-English Lexicon*, s.v. ἐνέργεια.

3. Bradshaw, who studied *energeia* from Aristotle to Medieval times in East and West, writes that Aristotle defined *energeia* as "the exercise of a capacity in contrast to its mere possession." Bradshaw, *Aristotle East and West*, 3.

4. See Lampe, *Patristic Greek Lexicon*, s.v. ἐνέργεια.

Energeia *and* Theopoiēsis

Activity (*energeia*) of the Trinity

Athanasius clarifies the meaning of divine *energeia* through many examples. He talks about God's guidance leading the Israelites out of Egypt: "For God himself through the Word in the Spirit guided the people."[5] By the expressions "through" the Word and "in" the Spirit Athanasius is saying the activity of guidance was undertaken by the whole Trinity. He uses the same expressions to speak about God's presence: "For when the Spirit was among the people, God was among them through the Son in the Spirit."[6] Any activity undertaken by the Godhead is understood as an activity of the whole Trinity in which each person of the Trinity participates equally in oneness (*enotētos*) as expressed by the formula "From the Father, Through the Son, In the Holy Spirit." When Scripture says "I led you out of the land of Egypt," the "I" refers to the one Godhead doing the one activity of "leading," which when viewed through a Trinitarian lens becomes "For God himself through the Word in the Spirit guided the people." This expression does not divide the Trinity but unites it. Athanasius affirms the indivisibility and oneness (*enotētos*) of the Trinity: "There is such an order and unity [*enotētos*] in the Holy Trinity, who could separate either the Son from the Father, or the Spirit from the Son or from the Father himself?"[7]

Energeia as expressed in Athanasius's formula "from, through, in" preserves the oneness of the Trinity. Athanasius opposes the Arian and Tropikoi heresies that claim the

5. *Ep. Serap.* 1.12.4.

6. *Ep. Serap.* 1.12.5.

7. *Ep. Serap.* 1.20.1. Bradshaw quotes Aristotle, "that which is composite and divisible into parts has several different activities, but that which is by nature simple and whose being does not consist in relation to something else must have only one excellence in the full sense of the word." Bradshaw, *Aristotle East and West*, 4.

Son and the Holy Spirit are created beings. "Because they cannot understand how the Holy Trinity is indivisible, the Arians make the Son one with the created order, and the Tropikoi themselves classify the Spirit with the creatures."[8] Athanasius responds that if any person of the Trinity were a created being, that person would be foreign and external to the Trinity. The Trinity is not composed of Creator and creature; on the contrary, the Trinity is the Creator and Maker. The Trinity is indivisible, holy, and perfect, and confessed as Father, Son, and Holy Spirit. "The Father does all things through the Word in the Holy Spirit. In this way the unity (*ēenotēs*) of the Trinity is preserved, and in this way is the one God preached in the Church, *who is above all and through all and in all* (Eph 4:6)—*above all* as Father, as beginning, as source; *through all*, through the Word; *in all*, in the Holy Spirit. It is not a Trinity in name alone and in linguistic expression, but in truth and actual existence."[9] Athanasius argues that if the oneness of the *energeia* is not preserved, some could claim it is only the Father who is the creator while the Son and Holy Spirit are created beings, and this would affect the Trinity since creation would be an act of the Father. Athanasius also writes, "the Father creates and renews all thing through the Word in the Holy Spirit."[10] Adding the concept of the oneness of the *energeia* to the idea of the oneness of essence strengthens the unity of the Trinity.

Paul taught the oneness (*enotēta*) of the Trinity when he wrote in 1 Corinthians 12:4-6, "Now there are varieties of gifts, but the same Spirit; and there are varieties of services, but the same Lord; and there are varieties of activities [*energēmatōn*], but it is the same God who activates

8. *Ep. Serap.* 1.17.4.
9. *Ep. Serap.* 1.28.2-3.
10. *Ep. Serap.* 1.24.6.

[*energōn*] all of them in everyone." Athanasius expresses the activity of the Trinity in this verse by writing that the Spirit distributed the gifts "bestowed by the Father through the Word. For all the Father has is the Son's. Thus what is given by the Son in the Spirit is a gift of the Father."[11] Athanasius expresses the oneness of the activity in 2 Corinthians 13:13—"The grace of the Lord Jesus Christ, the love of God, and the communion of [a] the Holy Spirit be with all of you"—by writing that "this grace and gift given in the Trinity is given by the Father through the Son in the Holy Spirit."[12] What is under discussion here is the activity of bestowing of gifts. Though there are a variety of gifts, the activity of bestowing them by the Trinity is one. Athanasius concludes his explanation: "There is one activity of the Trinity. The Apostle does not mean that the gifts given by each are different and distinct, but that whatever gift is given is given in the Trinity, and that all the gifts are from the one God."[13]

The activity of prophecy and the incarnation both come about through the Trinity acting in oneness. When sacred writers say, "'Thus says the Lord,' they are not speaking otherwise than in the Holy Spirit, and when they speak in the Spirit, whatever it is they say, they say it in Christ."[14] Similarly, the Word in the Spirit visited the Virgin Mary and "formed the body and accommodated it to himself." The incarnation is the Word taking the body as his own to the Father through the Word in the Spirit.[15] Athanasius comments on the true worshipers mentioned in the story of the Samaritan woman in John 4: "True worshipers worship the

11. *Ep. Serap.* 1.30.4.
12. *Ep. Serap.* 1.30.6.
13. *Ep. Serap.* 1.31.1.
14. *Ep. Serap.* 1.31.11.
15. *Ep. Serap.* 1.31.12.

Father but in Spirit and Truth, confessing the Son and the Spirit who is in him. For the Spirit is inseparable from the Son, just as the Son is inseparable from the Father."[16] In all of these examples, Athanasius asserts the oneness of activity of the Trinity regarding ancient prophecy, in the incarnation, and interaction with humanity during his economy. Athanasius explains all actions of the Godhead with creation and created beings are from the Father, through the Son, in the Holy Spirit. The Trinity is indivisible and always acting in oneness.

Baptism is also an activity of the Trinity. If baptism were not performed through a oneness of *energeia*—that is, in the name of the Father, Son, and Holy Spirit—and in the name of only one person of the Trinity, then the baptized is not initiated into the Godhead since baptism is initiation into the Trinity.[17] The Trinity is indivisible, eternal, and immutable in nature, and has one holiness; that is why baptism is in the name of the Trinity.

Athanasius argues from the oneness of activity to the oneness of essence. When Paul sends his greetings to the Romans, "Grace to you and peace from God our Father and the Lord Jesus Christ," the same grace and peace that was sent by the Father was sent by the Son.[18] While the light of the sun and its radiance are one, and the sun's illumination is affected by the radiance, the source of all is the sun. Similarly, there are not two sources of grace but it is the Father who gives grace and peace through the Son. When the Son works it is the Father who is the worker. When the Father speaks to the prophets, he speaks through the Son. If the Son and the Father were not of the same essence, such activity would have two different sources, and we would not

16. *Ep. Serap.* 1.33.4.
17. *Ep. Serap.* 1.30.1, 2.
18. Rom 1:7.

have only one God.[19] If it were only the Father who gives grace, or if he were the only giver, one would conclude that it is only the Father who is unoriginate and consequently the giver of all things. It is the mode of giving, the oneness of the activity, that demonstrates that the Father, Son, and Holy Spirit are of the same essence.[20] It is critical to highlight the one source of gifts. Gifts may vary, but the source and the giver of the gift is one and the activity of giving it is in oneness.

Athanasius also argues from the practice of worship, explaining that we do not ask to be given blessings or gifts from "God and the angels," but rather we pray to receive blessings from the Father and the Son because of their oneness (*enotēta*) and the oneness of their giving. We are given grace through the Son. All the Father's activity is through the Son, and it is through the Son that we are given what is given.[21] The angels minister at the command of God, they are sent forth with a mission that God sends them to complete; they do not initiate the mission but complete the command.[22] As created beings, angels are not a creative (*poiētikon*) cause, they are not of the essence of God, and do not give grace. Angels are ministering spirits sent to serve.[23] They are heralds of the gifts given from the Father through the Word. An angel was sent to Zacharias, another was sent to Mary the Theotokos; both Zacharias and Mary recognized that it was an angel they saw and not God or his Word.[24] Angels do the work (*ergon*) of God through their ministry and service but are not the *energeia* of God since

19. *C. Ar.* 3.11.
20. *C. Ar.* 3.12.
21. *C. Ar.* 3.12.
22. *C. Ar.* 3.12.
23. Heb 1:14.
24. *C. Ar.* 3.14.

they are external to God and of a different essence. Angels, as created beings, are not a creative cause of *energeia*.

The one *energeia* unites the Trinity, for it is an indication of the one essence of the Trinity. For the Father permeates all things, and He acts (*energein*) in all things through the Word in the Spirit.[25] Christians do not profess three gods or three origins; otherwise, Athanasius argues, he would have suggested the image of three suns. He always provides the example of a single sun with its radiance: the light is from the sun in the radiance. This example makes it clear there is only one origin, the sun. There is one Word from the one God for the Son is not external to the Father; for neither the Son nor the Holy Spirit is a creature. Christians confess God through the Trinity, which is distinct from other gods that are of many kinds and many parts.[26] If the Christian god were composed of many parts each would have its different and distinct nature and activity.[27] *Energeia* speaks about the creative essence of God. When the Divine says, "Let there be light" there is light. The pronouncement has a creative power that lasts forever. The Trinity has one creative *energeia*.

---

25. *C. Ar.* 3.15.

26. *C. Ar.* 3.15.

27. *C. Ar.* 3.15. Bradshaw's *Aristotle East and West* focuses on the divine activity and its relationship to God's being or essence in East and West and how this illuminates some of the theological differences between Eastern and Western churches. The study does not discuss *energeia* of the incarnate Son, nor does it mention Athanasius, but only gives a brief philosophical and theological history of divine *enregeia*. Athanasopoulos and Schneider, *Divine Essence and Divine Energies*, should be considered a critical response to Bradshaw's study.

Human Activity (energeia)

Athanasius compares the *energeia* of humans with that of God. The word of a human person does not have the power to create or produce activity. Humans are created out of nothing and it is not of their nature for their words to have creative power. Created humanity does not have such creative power in their words. Humans cannot transform water into wine with their human words. Neither human words nor human activity has creative power; they are temporal. The word of humans neither lives nor activates anything. On the other hand, God's Word has creative power, gives life, and has *energeia* to do anything.[28] In Athanasius's opinion, created beings do not have an *energeia* comparable with that of the divine, for human *energeia* is temporal and relevant to the present and ends with time.

Activity (energeia) of the Incarnate Son

Athanasius discusses another type of *energeia*: the *energeia* of the incarnate Son. As the *energeia* of the divinity is undivided and the whole Trinity acts in oneness, so is the *energeia* of the incarnate Son. Athanasius writes that when Christians worship the Son, we worship the Lord of creation, the Word of God, and the incarnate Word of God. The flesh is created but in the incarnation of the Word the body became God's own. In worship, we do not divide the body from the Word and worship it in itself or worship the Word apart from the body that he took as his own. Though the Word became flesh we still know and worship him as Lord.[29] The leper knew he was the Lord and worshiped him in the body, saying to him, "'Lord, if you choose, you can

---

28. *C. Ar.* 2.35.
29. *Ep. Adelph.* 3.

make me clean.' He stretched out his hand and touched him, saying, 'I do choose. Be made clean!' Immediately his leprosy was cleansed."[30] Similarly, the "woman who was suffering from hemorrhages for twelve years came up behind him and touched the fringe of his cloak, for she said to herself, 'If I only touch his cloak, I will be made well.' Jesus turned, and seeing her he said, 'Take heart, daughter; your faith has made you well.' And instantly the woman was made well."[31] In another example, when the waves of the raging sea heard the incarnate Word rebuke them, they became still and the storm ceased: "Then he got up and rebuked the winds and the sea; and there was a dead calm."[32] Furthermore, the man born blind was healed by the fleshly spitting of the incarnate Word, for "he spat on the ground and made mud with the saliva and spread the mud on the man's eyes."[33] In another example, where the only apparent aspect of the incarnate Word is the humanity, creation knew it was the Lord of creation who was on the cross and "the sun was darkened and the earth shook, the rocks were rent, and the veil of the temple rent, and many bodies of the saints which slept arose."[34] Not only that, but by stretching his hands on the cross and through the resurrection he overcame death.[35] Athanasius concludes, "he that dishonors the Temple dishonors the Lord in the Temple, and he that separates the Word from the body, sets at naught the grace given to us in Him."[36] Athanasius asserts in all of these examples, the worship is not divided

30. Matt 8:2–3.
31. Matt 9:20–22.
32. Matt 8:26.
33. John 9:6.
34. *Ep. Adelph.* 3.
35. *Ep. Adelph.* 6.
36. *Ep. Adelph.* 8.

Energeia *and* Theopoiēsis

since the divinity and the humanity cannot be separated. It is interesting that, among all these examples, Athanasius did not introduce Eucharistic worship. His successor, Cyril of Alexandria, elaborates on the oneness of worship of the humanity and divinity in the Eucharist; it will be a major point in the Nestorian controversy.

The common thread among these miracles is the oneness of the *energeia*. These miracles are significant for Athanasius's argument as he mentions them in more than one place in his writings. In the miracle of healing of the leper, the Gospel says "He stretched out his hand and touched him, saying, 'I do choose. Be made clean!'" The act of healing included Christ stretching out his hand, Christ's human hand touching the leper, and Christ's human voice pronouncing the command to be made clean. In the healing of Peter's mother-in-law he "took her by the hand and lifted her up"—here the miracle of healing included a physical touching of the hand, a human involvement in the act of divine healing. Athanasius explains, "He stretched forth His hand humanly, but He stopped the illness divinely."[37] In the miracle of raising Lazarus from the dead, Athanasius observes that when Christ went to Lazarus's tomb, it was the human voice that was the public declaration of the miracle of raising Lazarus and through it the miracle happened, "When he had said this, he cried with a loud voice, 'Lazarus, come out!' The dead man came out." Athanasius writes, "He gave forth a human voice as man; but divinely, as God, did He raise Lazarus from the dead."[38] There was no time interval between the touching and the healing or the raising from the dead. It represents one activity of healing and raising. It is no coincidence that such details are carefully documented in Scripture; they have a specific

37. Mark 1:31; *C. Ar.* 3.32.
38. John 11:43–44; *Ep. Adelph.* 7; *C. Ar.* 3.32.

theological significance. They document the one *energeia* of the incarnate Son, in which his divine act of healing was carried out through the humanity that he took as his own; thus, the one Jesus Christ is performing his activity in oneness of the humanity and divinity. Athanasius demonstrates the oneness of *energeia* of the incarnate Son in this miracle and the rest of the miracles on his list. This consistent line of thought regarding the oneness of activity of the incarnate Son is picked up by Cyril of Alexandria, who expands and reflects on more miracles, such as the healing of the son of the widow of Nain.[39] Cyril of Alexandria also uses the understanding that Christ took a human body and made it his own and the oneness of activity of the incarnate Son in both the Nestorian debate and Eucharistic theology.

By the early seventh century the concept of *monoenergism* (one *energeia*) was suggested as a way to end the rift between the Chalcedonians and non-Chalcedonians that occurred in 451. It was intended that both parties would agree there are two natures in the incarnate Son united by one *energeia*, though the terms "one" and "*energeia*" were not clearly defined. The proposal was opposed so the concept of *monotheletism* ("one will") was suggested instead. Later, *energeia* became a theological topic in Byzantine orthodoxy through the writings of Gregory Palamas, a fourteenth-century Byzantine theologian. The Latin West, represented by Thomas Aquinas, did not accept Palamas's *energeia* as distinct from the essence of God. Within the Alexandrian tradition, Cyril of Alexandria developed the concept of *energeia* based on the foundations that Athanasius had laid down in his writings. Timothy II of Alexandria developed the concept further in the fifth century based on Cyril's work. The term *energeia* acquired theological and historical significance much later than the time of

39. Luke 7:14.

THEOPOIĒSIS: MAKING DIVINE

Athanasius concludes his seminal two-volume work *Against the Pagans—On the Incarnation* with his famous and most quoted dictum: "For he became human that we might be made god (*theopoiēthōmen*)."[40] Athanasius writes that it is hard to comprehend the breadth of the incarnation, which is beyond human understanding; with exceeding wonder one sees the divinity of the Word surrounding us everywhere.[41] It is with this wonder that Athanasius delves into *theopoiēsis*. Athanasius constantly uses the term *theopoiēsis*, which is of his own coinage, to explain the incorruptibility and renewal granted to humanity by the incarnation. The literal meaning of *theopoieō* is to "make into a god,"[42] and *theopoiēsis* is "making divine."[43] This should not be confused with *theōsis*, which is translated as "deification" and "divinization."[44] *Theōsis* was coined by Gregory Nazianzus and became the standard term in Byzantine theology, and the most commonly used term in modern theological texts, to denote the various senses of deification represented in different theological traditions. "For Gregory of Nazianzus *theosis* is man's *telos* brought about on the one hand by the deifying power of the Holy Spirit in baptism, and on the other by the moral struggle in the ascetic life. But we can never bridge the gap between the created and uncreated

---

40. *Inc.* 54
41. *Inc.* 54.
42. See Lampe, *Patristic Greek Lexicon*, s.v. θεοποιέω, p. 630.
43. See Lampe, *Patristic Greek Lexicon*, s.v. θεοποίησις, p. 631.
44. See Lampe, *Patristic Greek Lexicon*, s.v. θέωσις, p. 649.

orders of reality."[45] The focus of this chapter is Athanasius of Alexandria's *theopoiēsis*.

Athanasius explains that when the Word became incarnate and took a body as his own, a body that was liable to death and corruption, he did so out of his lovingkindness for humanity. By body, Athanasius means the fullness of humanity: body, spirit, and a soul endowed with reason. He took the body and made it his own so that when he died on the cross, we all died in him, so that by his resurrection he would overcome death and corruption. The overcoming of death and corruption was completed in the Lord's body, and the law of corruption in humanity was abolished. In his death we died with him and by his resurrection he granted humanity life and incorruption.[46] Through the incarnation he granted us renewal of life, restored the image of God within us, and granted us incorruption. He became human that we might be made god (*theopoiēthōmen*).

Theopoiēsis is an exaltation of humanity; it is different than but related to the exaltation of the incarnate Son, which was for our sake. Athanasius points out that the exaltation of the Son in Philippians 2:9–10 is not a reward by a deliberate act; if it were, it could be taken away the way it was given. Rather, the Son is exalted by nature and this is never altered because his sonship is by nature and not a gift.[47] He is always Son, Lord of glory and ever worshiped; he descended and became incarnate, not for his own promotion, but rather for our sakes, to make us children of the Father and gods.[48] Adoption cannot happen except through the real Son; similarly, being made God cannot happen except through the Word. We are not children by nature, but

45. Russell, *Doctrine of Deification*, 233.
46. *Inc.* 8.
47. *C. Ar.* 1.37.
48. *C. Ar.* 1.38.

were made children through the Son who is of the essence of the Father; in the same way, divinity is not part of created nature, but we were made gods through the Son. He was not first human and then became God, but he was first God and then became human to make us gods. For he is God by nature and according to essence.[49] The exaltation mentioned in Philippians 2:9–10 is not the exaltation of the Son, for he is God by nature, but it is the exaltation of humanity when we were made children and gods. The Son granted us what belongs to God: as the resurrection granted us renewal and restoration of the divine image within us, so we became sanctified, exalted, children of the most High, and gods. *Theopoiēsis* does not transform the nature of humanity, but renews, exalts, and sanctifies the human nature that Christ has taken as his own. When Christ appropriates, or takes as his own, the fullness of humanity, with all it entails, and overcomes death and corruption, we receive incorruption through him and are made gods; then *theopoiēsis* takes place.[50] Taking a body did not change or weaken the Word, but rather he made divine what he put on and gave it freely to humanity.[51] Humanity is clothed in the flesh in order to exist, but the Word of God became incarnate and took flesh as his own in order to sanctify the flesh.[52] We were dead, and through the incarnation we are "made alive" and become temples of God.[53] By making us alive, he makes life, he grants us the renewal of life.[54] Through his incarnation, humans are "made" children, "made" gods, "made" alive. It is the whole process of being "made" that is at the core

49. *C. Ar.* 1.39.
50. *C. Ar.* 1.41.
51. *C. Ar.* 1.42.
52. *C. Ar.* 2.10.
53. *C. Ar* 1.42.
54. *C. Ar* 1.59 (8); *C. Ar.* 1.60 (9).

of understanding *theopoiēsis*. It is the understanding that our created nature was exalted through the Son and made divine but not of the same essence as God.

As previously discussed, in his defense against the Arians, who claimed the Son was a created being before the incarnation, Athanasius insists that the Son is divine, and it is only after the incarnation and taking a body as his own that we can say the Son had a created body. So, what we read in Scripture of the Son eating, sleeping, and suffering pain and death, among other human activities, refers to the created body that he took as his own and not to the Son who is of the essence of the Father and fully divine. Thus the emphasis on aspects of the Son being "made" and "created" (*poieō*) becomes pivotal in the Arian controversy and should be understood within that context. Athanasius emphasizes "made" and "created" for the sake of preserving the divinity of the Son while preserving the fullness of the incarnation and showing that the Son took on humanity in truth. Athanasius writes, "For it is the same to say work or creature, so that the proof that He is no work is a proof also that He is no creature."[55] Athanasius observes that when the word "made" is applied, it is always applied to creatures. What is made has a beginning, and since God has no beginning then only created beings are "made."[56] What has a beginning is not part of the essence of the eternal creator but external to the creator. Thus John writes in the beginning "was" the Word; he does not write that the Word "became" or "was made," but simply that he "was," for he always was and eternally exists.[57] *Poieō* is used with created beings or objects. Athanasius is careful to say that people are made divine, not become divine. Being thus "made"

55. *C. Ar.* 2.18.
56. *C. Ar.* 2.57.
57. *C. Ar.* 2.58.

Energeia *and* Theopoiēsis

divine assures there is no change in the essence of humanity; while humans are made gods their essence remains that of created beings. The making divine is through the Son, the Creator, for humans do not become divinized by a transformation through or of their own inner essence. "Things originate are made and do not make; or else they made even themselves."[58] Divinization is given to created beings and is understood as an aspect of renewal. This is why the concept of renewal is so vital to Athanasius; it is the process of being made divine, among other things. What the incarnation granted to humanity is the fullness of renewal, the fullness of being in God's image, which we lost by our transgression, the overcoming of death and being made incorruptible, and being made god. The incarnation does not transform the essence of human nature but aims to perfect it to its initial glory when God created it in his own image and declared it to be perfect. *Theopoiēsis* is the process of bringing humanity back to the fullness of Christ, to be the ultimate human being created in God's image. It is not to transform human nature into the divine essence, but to bring humans to the fullness of humanity, the fullness of renewal, the fullness of being perfect human beings who are created in the image of the divine and who do not suffer death any longer as they are made incorruptible.

Athanasius explains that when John writes the Word was made flesh, no one thinks the whole Word was made flesh, but rather the Word put on flesh and became incarnate. The Word took this created body for our sake, so that in him we are able to be renewed (*anakainisthēnai*) and are made gods (*theopoiēthēnai*).[59] The process of renewal can only be granted through the body that the Word took as his own. Because the Word, who is of the Father, took a human

58. *Ep. Afr.* 7.
59. *C. Ar.* 2.47.

body as his own we have communion with the divine and are able to be made divine and incorruptible. Because the Son is the true God, and not a creature, humanity is made divine. Through the incarnation what is divine by nature joined what is created by nature so that humanity might be saved, sanctified, and made divine.[60] God created us through the Word, so we are creatures by nature, but through the incarnation, we are made children of God and God the Creator becomes our Father. We are children by adoption not by nature and it is only through the Word, who is in us, that we cry to the Father and say "Abba Father."[61] Through the incarnate Son, created humans are made sons (*uiopoieitai*).[62] Similarly, we are not gods by nature but it is through the incarnation, through the Son who is in us, who sanctifies us, that we are made gods.

Theopoiēsis grants us incorruptibility and other attributes of the Divine. We are asked to be merciful as the Father in heaven is merciful and we are asked to be perfect as our heavenly Father is perfect.[63] Neither our merciful actions towards others nor our progress towards perfection will make us equal to God in mercy and perfection. It is through grace that we are given to be merciful, perfect, and children of the Most High. We are called gods through his grace: we are not equal to the true God or his Word, but through his grace we become merciful. We do not become in nature benefactors or equal to God, but what has been given to us by God through grace we impart to all humanity, so we become imitators of God. When we become children of the Father we partake of his Spirit, we become virtuous, imitators, and children of God. This does not make us equal

60. *C. Ar.* 2.70.
61. *C. Ar.* 2.59.
62. *C. Ar.* 2.64.
63. Luke 6:36; Matt 5:48.

Energeia *and* Theopoiēsis

to God but gives us the oneness of the Spirit the children of God ought to have.[64] As imitators of the divine we have divine attributes that make us gods. We are merciful as the Father is merciful, but we are not the Father himself. We are sons and gods, but not like the Son or God himself.[65] We are imitators of God in being united in oneness by being one "in us [the Father and the Son]."[66] Athanasius clarifies that our unity imitates the oneness of the Son and the Father but we are not in the Father in the same way as the Son is in the Father. Only the Son is in the Father, but we are in the Son and through him in the Father.[67] We are learning our unity by imitation from the oneness of the Father and Son. These are examples to help us understand how we are made divine when we imitate God in mercy, perfection, and living in unity with one another as the Son is in oneness with the Father. We can never be equal to God in his mercy or perfection, nor can we live in unity as the Son is in the Father, but being imitators of the divine, imitators of his perfection and mercy, the Divine makes us gods.

To be made gods does not change our essence as humans. The Word became flesh, and took a body as his own so that when he sanctifies this body, we are sanctified in him and made gods. Without the incarnation we cannot receive the gift of deification, for it is through the incarnate Word that we are made gods. When we receive this gift our essence does not change into a divine essence just as the essence of the Word did not change when the Word became flesh but rather it deified the body and rendered it

64. *C. Ar.* 3.19.

65. *C. Ar.* 3.20.

66. ". . . that they may all be one. As you, Father, are in me and I am in you, may they also be in us, so that the world may believe that you have sent me" (John 17:21).

67. *C. Ar.* 3.21, 25.

immortal.[68] Just as we are "made children of God" though our essence does not change—we are not of the same essence as the Son of God—we are made gods though the essence of our humanity does not change.[69]

If the essence of the Son is not divine like that of the Father he cannot be the enlightening power of the Father nor have the power to make us gods. If the Son is not God himself he cannot make us gods. He is the power of the Father and when we partake of the Son we partake of the Father himself. Because he is of the essence of the Father all things come to life through him and through him we are made gods. If the Son makes us gods there is no doubt that his nature is divine.[70]

It is through the incarnation that humans are made gods. When the Word took flesh with all its properties and made it his own—all the works of the Godhead of the Word were done through the body—humanity was delivered from corruption and we were made gods. What the incarnation granted humanity is different from the sanctification previously given to people such as Jeremiah or John the Baptist, who were both sanctified in the womb yet died like the rest, for death reigned over all humanity. These examples demonstrate that no aspect of sanctification given to humanity before the incarnation could stop the corruption and mortality in human nature. It was only after the incarnation, when Christ overcame death with his resurrection, that humanity was granted incorruption and immortality. When the Word became human and appropriated all that belongs to humanity as his own, he destroyed corruption and granted humanity eternal life. We are no longer earthly

68. *Decr.* 14.
69. *Decr.* 31.
70. *Syn.* 51; *Ep. Serap.* 1.24.1.

Energeia *and* Theopoiēsis

but regenerated by water and the Spirit, and in Christ and with Christ we rise to eternal life.[71]

Athanasius argues that Christ has taken a body like ours so that what he secures for himself in the flesh is secured for humanity for eternity; it cannot be taken away from us. The flesh that Christ took as his own bore all the weaknesses of human nature, such as thirst, hunger, ignorance, suffering, and death. At the same time, this very same flesh raised the dead and healed the sick. All the questions he asked in his humanity, which might show ignorance, were asked to vouchsafe knowledge of the Father for our sake. Whatever Christ received in the flesh, he received for our sake. Whatever men receive can be lost, as in the case of Adam, but what Christ received in the flesh is irrevocable and is secure for humanity.[72] The Word became flesh so that what he receives in that flesh, humanity receives; he became flesh to sanctify us and make us gods.[73] When he was washed in the Jordan, we were washed in him and by him. When the Spirit descended on him in the Jordan, it descended on us; it was we who were the recipients of the Spirit. The body that was sanctified is his, and from him we became sanctified.[74] When the Word became flesh and made it his own, all the ways the flesh was perfected became ours.[75] The advancements of the flesh are not external to the flesh, for the flesh was his own, nor were they promotion to the Godhead. The advances in the flesh and deification of the flesh are for our sake, for humanity to receive them.[76] The Word became flesh to overcome demons and death; and as we

71. *C. Ar.* 3.33.
72. *C. Ar.* 3.38.
73. *C. Ar.* 3.39; *Ep. Adelph.* 4.
74. *C. Ar.* 1.47.
75. *C. Ar.* 3.53.
76. *C. Ar.* 3.53.

became partakers of divine nature, we overcome demons and death, we are liberated from corruption.[77] Whatever Christ does, he does for our sake. After the resurrection, the risen flesh has overcome mortality and become deified so that what Christ has secured in his own flesh becomes ours.[78] The Word by its own free will accepted death in the flesh on our behalf. The flesh fears death, and he willingly accepted the fear of death on our behalf to overcome the fear of death in humanity. Because he overcame the fear of death and death itself with his resurrection, Christians now are prepared to face death without fear.[79] Humanity is mortal; it does not die by its own free will but by the necessity of its mortal nature. The Son being immortal took mortal flesh as his own, but by his power as God the mortal flesh becomes immortal because the Word who assumed it preserved it incorruptible so that we partake of immortality from him.[80] Whatever the Son has secured in his flesh he secured for humanity. He secured knowledge of the Father and the descent of the Spirit on us. He secured immortality and incorruption. This advancement and exaltation granted to us by the Son's incarnation are secured by the Son and cannot be taken away from us.

In summary, Athanasius's dictum, "for he became human that we might be made god (*theopoiēthōmen*)" summarizes the essence of our salvation.[81] The Son of God became incarnate and took to himself a body as his own, a body that represents the fullness of the human essence and all that humanity is. He carried all the infirmities of humanity as his own: our mortality, fear, suffering, and all weakness that

77. *C. Ar.* 3.40.
78. *C. Ar.* 3.48.
79. *C. Ar.* 3.57.
80. *C. Ar.* 3.57.
81. *Inc.* 54.

Energeia and Theopoiēsis

characterizes human nature. Through his divine nature he advances the human condition and heals our sickness. He made us children of God and we are able to call God "our Father." He cleansed us in the river Jordan and accepted the Spirit on our behalf so that through him and in him we are sanctified. He took away the fear of death and gave us eternal life and immortality by overcoming death with his death. It is immortality and incorruption that seal the understanding that we are made gods, for only God is immortal. If the Son is not fully divine we could not have been sanctified and been made gods. This gift does not change either his nature or the nature of humanity. Through the incarnation and by the power of his resurrection humanity was granted renewal, the renewal of God's image within us, and *theopoiēsis*. Athanasius adds a Eucharistic dimension to the understanding of *theopoiēsis* for we are made gods by partaking of the body of the Word himself.[82]

Athanasius discusses in his writings three aspects of *energeia*. He discusses the divine *energeia* that characterizes the activity of the Trinity. He gives many examples to demonstrate that any divine activity is from the Father through the Son in the Holy Spirit. Divine *energeia* assures the oneness of the Trinity and the oneness of the essence. With this theological principle, Athanasius argues that the Son and the Holy Spirit must be divine. If the Son is a created being and his activity is introduced in the Trinity then the Son is external and we have a fourth person introduced to the Trinity. The same applies to the Holy Spirit. Athanasius briefly discusses human activity, which is temporal, does not have creative power, and cannot be compared to that of the divine. He then discusses the *energeia* of the incarnate Son, demonstrating through a series of examples of miracles in which Christ acts in oneness of the humanity and

---

82. *Ep. Max.* 2.

the divinity, each participating in each activity Christ has undertaken. Athanasius here asserts that, as *energeia* unites and assures oneness of the Godhead, the oneness of the activity of the incarnate Son assures the oneness of the person of Christ. Thus *energeia* unites the three persons of the Trinity, and *energeia* unites the two natures of the incarnate Son. Athanasius does not go further, however, to conclude the oneness of the Son preserves the oneness of the Trinity, or if the incarnate Son has two separate activities, the unity of the Trinity will be in jeopardy. Though this conclusion is straightforwardly deduced, he never spells it out. This is developed by Cyril of Alexandria during the debates of the Nestorian controversy who will argue that to preserve the oneness of the Trinity the activity of the incarnate Son must be in oneness.[83]

Energeia and *theopoiēsis* are two concepts Athanasius applied in his understanding of the Divine essence and the understanding of our salvation. *Energeia* has not taken much traction in western theology, while Byzantine theology focused primarily on divine *energeia*. This chapter made clear the significance and specificity of Athanasius's understanding of *energeia* and that it should not be confused with later developments. *Theopoiēsis* attracted more interest once it was subsumed under the term *theosis* coined by Gregory of Nazianzus. It should be noted that Athanasius never used the term *theosis* in his writings and therefore we should recognize the distinctiveness of the concept of *theopoiēsis* that he introduced and it should be understood on his own terms.

---

83. "The identity of activity among the three persons indicates identity of being; this becomes a fundamental principle of the Trinitarian theology of Cyril of Alexandria as well as of the Cappadocians." Anatolios, *Athanasius*, 277.

Energeia *and* Theopoiēsis

QUESTIONS FOR FURTHER DISCUSSION

- How does the concept of oneness of energeia cement the oneness of the Trinity and the oneness of its essence?
- How does Athanasius's formula "from, through, in" preserves the oneness of the Trinity?
- How does Athanasius explain the oneness of the activity of the incarnate Son?
- What does "For he became human that we might be made god (theopoiēthōmen)" mean? How are humans made god?

SUGGESTIONS FOR FURTHER READING

Orations against the Arians 3:11–15; 30–35
Orations against the Arians 1:38–45; 2:47, 59, 70; 3:19–53
Letters to Serapion concerning the Holy Spirit 1.12–33
Letter to Adelphius (especially 60:4)

6

THE SPIRITUAL LIFE, A LIFE OF RENEWAL

SPIRITUALITY IN ATHANASIUS'S WRITINGS is theologically founded on the life of renewal the incarnation granted humanity: the renewal of God's image and *theopoiēsis*. These theological themes are biblically based and woven together with a sense of practicality and simplicity. Athanasian spirituality is based on the advancement of the spirituality of the person with the underlying premise that personal spiritual growth collectively changes the larger community and society. Though Athanasius's spiritual direction starts with the person, his *Festal Letters*, addressed to the whole church, reveal his pastoral spiritual advice to a larger audience. This chapter will begin with the theological foundations of Athanasian spirituality followed by the impact and practical application of this spiritual theology on first the personal level then the pastoral and collective level as exhibited in Athanasius's writings.

THE THEOLOGICAL FOUNDATION OF ATHANASIUS'S SPIRITUALITY

In one of his *Festal Letters* Athanasius observes that Paul gave different advice to different people as a model of adapting the message to the needs of every person. Paul always began, however, by preaching the word and the mystery of the Lord, that is, Paul always began with teaching the mysteries of the faith before asking his readers to change their way of life. For it is only when the people desire to live with Christ after knowing what Christ did for their salvation that people will easily follow what Christ commands.[1] Athanasius asserts the Evangelists followed the same pattern of teaching the faith then exhorting to virtue.[2] Athanasius advises that we first have to teach the Christian message to the people. When they know the message, they will naturally desire to live according to Christ's model. Athanasius believes spirituality is based on a strong biblical and theological foundation; only on such a foundation can a person pursue a spiritual life.

The theological foundation of Athanasius's spirituality can be gleaned from the double work *Against the Pagans—On the Incarnation* together with the *Life of Antony*.[3] *Against the Pagans* starts with fallen humanity. God created humanity through his own Word and in the image of the Word who is the Image of the invisible God. The immortal

1. *Ep. fest.* 11.2,3.
2. *Ep. fest.* 11.4.
3. This continues some aspects of the discussion in chapter 2. A more detailed exposition of Athanasius's spiritual theology is in Farag, *Balance of the Heart*, 47–94.

soul is endowed with reason through which it contemplates and beholds God, has within itself the knowledge of the Word of God, and knows of its immortality. Humanity is created to live in blessedness and to contemplate God, guided by the soul that helps it reach the aim of its creation. It is through the purity of the soul that we can see God.[4] When we contemplate the Word, the Word guides us to preserve this purity since he is the Image of the Father after whose image humanity was made. When the human mind transcends the things of the body and the senses, it is raised high and takes pleasure in contemplating the Word and the Father and gains renewal. The aim of the spiritual life is to reach this state of mind where the soul is in constant contemplation of God without hindrance from the senses or anything else.

Being created in the image of the Word/Logos means the human soul is endowed with human reason and a *nous* that is always oriented towards the contemplation of God.[5] God dwells within us, for the kingdom of God is within us. Searching within ourselves we contemplate the Divine dwelling within us; we attend to the *nous* guiding our soul towards God himself. The *nous* that resides within the soul discerns the external temptations to the senses and decides what is best for the soul. When the body and its senses are quiet and still, the rational soul can behold what is beyond the immediate bodily senses and can behold and contemplate God.[6] The awareness of the immortality of the soul inclines human beings to seek virtue even in the face of physical harm or even death.[7] The movement of the soul does not cease with the death of the body and thoughts of

4. Matt 5:8.
5. *C. Gent.* 19–21.
6. *C. Gent.* 30–31.
7. *C. Gent.* 32.

immortality never desert the soul, for the soul transcends the nature of the body and always yearns to contemplate God.[8]

Even endowed with all these gifts, people turned toward evil by conceiving evil in the imagination of their minds. God did not create evil. Athanasius rejects the idea of evil as an independent, created, substantive reality and does not attribute to matter the principle of evil. Matter, however, captivates the senses and there is a need for the constant discernment of the *nous* residing within the soul not to let matter overtake the soul. When humans chose to contemplate their bodies and all that belongs to the senses, they were deprived of the contemplation of divine things. They discovered they were naked, they learned to commit wrong, and they began to contemplate evil rather than God.[9] When the soul is away from God and the mind is not occupied with the contemplation of God, the soul loses its ability to distinguish between what is good and what is evil.

The fall took place when humans chose not to contemplate God. Their minds were drawn to the senses, to the created world and not to God. Humanity strayed and needed salvation. It was thus necessary for the Word, who created the world, to renew and save creation.[10] When humans transgressed the commandment and chose to eat from the tree, when they chose the material world over the contemplation of God, they suffered the consequence of the transgression and came under the sentence of death and corruption.[11] Humans could no longer live in eternity with God. But in his lovingkindness toward his creation the Word would not accept that creation should suffer death

8. *C. Gent.* 33.
9. *C. Gent.* 3.
10. *Inc.* 1.
11. *Inc.* 3.

and corruption and go to waste. Only death could undo the corruption of humanity.[12] Only God the Word was able to recreate and renew humanity. He was the only one who could suffer and die on behalf of the humanity made in his image. God the Word is incorporeal, incorruptible, and immaterial and does not die. God the Word became incarnate to die on our behalf. We are the object of his incarnation.[13] He took a body and made it his own. When he died on the cross, we died in him. When he overcame death by his resurrection we rose with him. He conquered death and overturned the sentence of corruption. Neither death nor corruption have a hold on humanity. "He became human that we might be made god (*theopoiēthōmen*)."[14]

The Word overcame death by his resurrection, renewed humanity, and renewed God's image within humanity. Humans became immortal, were made god, and came to know God the Father, worship him, and call him "Abba." Knowing God makes us seek the contemplation of God, makes us seek virtue of the soul. The incarnation gave us power to transcend the body and seek what is beyond the senses. By the incarnation, humans can perceive the unseen Father and contemplate God. The incarnate Word gave humanity the life of renewal.

What has been presented here represents the high points of Athanasius's understanding of salvation of the human person, from the source of evil and the fall to the incarnation and resurrection, the renewal of life, the renewal of God's image within humanity, and *theopoiēsis*. All these theological themes form the core of the spiritual life, whether of the person or of the Christian community. Athanasius does not believe this spiritual life is merely theoretical or

12. *Inc.* 5, 9.
13. *Inc.* 4.
14. *Inc.* 54.

unattainable; rather, it is how to live as a Christian. The *Life of Antony* is a demonstration of the life of renewal, of a life according to the new creation that Christians became with the resurrection. The *Life of Antony* describes how the *nous* guides the soul to a life of prayer through the careful reading of Scripture and renouncing all things for the sake of constant contemplation of God. The spiritual life that Athanasius charted in *Against the Pagans—On the Incarnation* and the *Life of Antony* depicts how the soul lived in deep contemplation of God and then forsook God for its senses. The Word, however, could not forsake his creation and became incarnate, saving humanity, overcoming death, and granting humans a renewed life, and a life of immortality. The *nous* is no longer blinded by the senses beyond its will, but rather is uplifted with power of the resurrection. There is nothing that hinders humanity from becoming the dwelling place of the Divine and living in constant contemplation of God. It is a spiritual life that surpasses the paradisiac state. It is a spiritual life characterized by joy at the Word's triumph over death, rejoicing in the Word, the giver of life. It is a spiritual life of humans living as children of God with the divine image renewed within them. It is a spiritual life rooted in the deep understanding of the incarnation and the true essence of salvation.

PERSONAL AND INDIVIDUAL SPIRITUALITY

The theological foundation of Alexandrian spirituality, as presented by Athanasius of Alexandria, is the interaction of the Divine with the *nous* and the soul of each human person. The incarnation and resurrection saved humanity but at the same time it is the story of salvation of each human person, each human soul, within the larger human body. Alexandrian spirituality addresses the salvation of each human person, each rational soul, that collectively constitute the larger Christian body and the church. A good example is Antony, who, though he lived in solitude, encouraged many to follow a more spiritual life through the many spiritual advances he gained in his solitary life. Many men chose to stay with him and emulate his spiritual life, and others, both men and women, visited him seeking his spiritual guidance. Antony's spiritual life radiated beyond his solitary confinement.[15] Alexandrian spirituality believes that the seed of one person gives fruit to many. The example of one is a statement of mission to the many who encounter the person living this spiritual life. Thus, Athanasius is attentive to personal spirituality because it is the foundation of the spirituality of the larger Christian body.

Athanasius describes the spiritual life of a Christian in one of his *Festal Letters*. The righteous become disciples of the kingdom of heaven and are in constant meditation on Scripture, whether they are sitting, walking, or in any other activity.[16] The Christian becomes grounded in the faith, rejoicing in hope, and bold in the spirit. The thoughts of the mind move the Christian to act in virtue. For everything starts with the thoughts of the mind. Christ taught whoever looks at a woman with lust has committed adultery, and whoever is angry with his brother has committed murder.[17] If the thought of the mind did not have wrath there would have been no murder and if the thought of the mind had no lust there would be no adultery. If one keeps meditating on the word of God the mind will be conversing with

---

15. This segment continues the discussion in chapter 2, section "Antony, an Exemplar of the Life of Renewal."

16. Deut 6:7.

17. Matt 5:22, 28.

The Spiritual Life, a Life of Renewal

virtue and the person will act in righteousness.[18] Athanasius continues,

> Worthy of admiration is the virtue of that man, my brethren! for through Timothy he enjoins upon all, that they should have regard to nothing more than to godliness, but above everything to adjudge the chief place to faith in God. For what grace has the unrighteous man, though he may feign to keep the commandments? Nay rather, the unrighteous man is unable even to keep a portion of the law, for as is his mind, such of necessity must be his actions; as the Spirit says, reproving such; "The fool hath said in his heart, there is no God." After this the Word, shewing that actions correspond with thoughts, says, "They are corrupt; they are profane in their machinations." The unrighteous man then, in every respect corrupts his body; stealing, committing adultery, cursing, being drunken, and doing such like things.[19]

Athanasius confirms it is the thought/*nous* anchored in faith that guides the person to righteousness. We observe again the theme of the mind/*nous* guiding the soul and the person toward the life of virtue.

In his *Letter to Marcellinus on the Interpretation of the Psalms* Athanasius addresses the topic of prayer using the psalms. The Psalms, he says, are different from the rest of Scripture. In Scripture one learns the commandments that guide the behavior, what to do or not do. Scripture also records the actions of the prophets and prophecies about the Savior. The Psalms relay similar themes but the reader "also comprehends and is taught in [them] the emotions of the

18. *Ep. fest.* 11.7.
19. *Ep. fest.* 11.8.

soul" and receives images "deriving from the words."[20] The Psalms teach not only repentance, but how to repent and what one must say while repenting. The Psalms teach not only to bear suffering but what to say during and after one is delivered from suffering. The Psalms teach to give thanks and what to say when giving thanks. The Psalms teach that one will be persecuted for living a godly life, and they provide the words to say while suffering persecution or fleeing from one's enemies, and after being delivered from one's suffering. The Psalms teach how to praise the Lord.[21] The Psalms teach the "emotions and dispositions of the souls, finding in them also the therapy and correction suited for each emotion."[22] The Psalms express the emotions of the soul going through various life experiences, whether joyous or sorrowful, and give the words to speak to God about them. The Psalms give words for repentance, suffering, thanksgiving, or praise and blessing. The Psalms give one the words for prayer and help one make the words one's own.[23] The one who hears the Psalms "is deeply moved, as though he himself were speaking, and is affected by the words of the songs, as if they were his own songs."[24] It is clear from Athanasius's description that the Psalms were chanted rather than read. Athanasius thinks it is fitting to praise God not "in compressed speech alone, but also in the voice that is richly broadened." Psalms are not just for the ear's delight, they are for the sake of praising the Lord. In addition, voices coming together into a single harmonious sound "appear in the soul" in their different movements,

20. *Ep. Marcell.* 10. All citations are from Athanasius, *Life of Antony and the Letter to Marcellinus*.
21. *Ep. Marcell.* 10.
22. *Ep. Marcell.* 13.
23. *Ep. Marcell.* 10, 11.
24. *Ep. Marcell.* 11.

affecting the activity of parts of the body to create harmony within a person.[25] Athanasius believes psalm chanting has a soothing and remedial effect on the soul and body through the power of the words and melodic rhythms. Athanasius maintains chanting the psalms should be with the mind and come from the soul that is in accord with the Spirit. Chanting should not be for the sake of good musical harmony but rather a "sign of the harmony of the soul's reflection. Indeed, the melodic reading is a symbol of the mind's well-ordered and undisturbed condition."[26] For Athanasius, chanting the psalms involves the whole person, soul, mind, and body. This reflects Athanasius's understanding of the human person and its composition and the role of the soul and mind/*nous* in his theology of salvation and the whole spiritual endeavor.

Athanasius's spiritual instruction is addressed primarily to the individual. It is based on his understanding of the human person and the role of mind/*nous* in guiding the soul toward divine contemplation. Whether it is the instruction on prayer and the reading of Scripture from the life of Antony or on praying and chanting the psalms, everything revolves around living the life of renewal granted to us by the incarnation and resurrection.

PASTORAL AND CORPORATE SPIRITUALITY

Athanasius, famous for his extensive theological refutation of the Arians, believes that "the faith of simplicity is better than an elaborate process of persuasion"; he was forced by circumstances to write elaborate treatises of persuasion to show the truth to the faithful.[27] As a pastor he preferred

25. *Ep. Marcell.* 27.
26. *Ep. Marcell.* 29.
27. *C. Ar.* 3.1.

the faith of simplicity but as a theologian he was obligated to defend the truth. As a pastor in frequent exiles in defense of the faith, he was responsible for a flock who equally endured persecution to defend that same faith. The faithful were attacked while attending church, their churches were confiscated by imperial decrees, they suffered loss of property, and they were persecuted for not accepting Arian teaching. It is within the context of the exile of Athanasius and the suffering of his flock that many of the *Festal Letters* were written and read in churches. It is within this context that Athanasius, the church leader, asks his flock to celebrate the feast in joy, to offer thanksgiving to God, to keep the faith and let it guide them to the life of virtue. It is from the *Festal Letters* that we can glean some of the pastoral and corporate aspects of Athanasius's spirituality.

Two main themes will be discussed: celebrating Passover and thanksgiving. Athanasius pays attention to the spiritual way that each person celebrates Passover but at the same time recognizes that it is a communal celebration. Athanasius asks, "For what else is the feast, but the constant worship of God, and the recognition of godliness, and unceasing prayers from the whole heart with agreement?" He then emphasizes, "Not therefore separately, but unitedly and collectively, let us all keep the feast together." He continues, "And the sacrifice is not offered in one place, but 'in every nation, incense and a pure sacrifice is offered unto God.'"[28] In another Festal Letter Athanasius writes from exile in Rome that he is keeping the feast with his flock because he and his people in Egypt are one in will and spirit, and they both send prayers in common to God.[29] Personal celebrations in unity create collective celebration. Athanasius

---

28. *Ep. fest.* 11.11, citing Mal 1:11.
29. *Ep. fest.* 13.1.

The Spiritual Life, a Life of Renewal

reminds his hearers that the Lord is the feast.[30] Therefore, the feast should not be an occasion for indulgence but a time to practice temperance and an occasion for virtue. It is the time to observe the purity of the fast, pray and read Scriptures, practice humility, take care of the poor, and make peace with one's enemy.[31] There is a practical aspect to celebrating Passover on the personal level that impacts the society. While attending to prayer and the study of Scripture are essential, peace and love within the larger Christian community are at the core of how to celebrate Passover.

The Passover celebration is preceded by a fast. Athanasius advises his flock to humble their souls during fasting.[32] He calls on his flock to sanctify the fast by not polluting the "thoughts of their hearts," not doing evil against their neighbors, and not boasting about their fast.[33] Athanasius is attentive to both the inner spiritual working of the thoughts of the heart and the outward, social interaction with one's neighbor with kindness and without boasting. Athanasius emphasizes that humility of soul is to characterize the fast and quotes Leviticus 23:29 that the soul that does not humble itself shall be cut off from the people.[34] In this public letter, addressed to all his people in Egypt and Libya, in his spiritual advice on fasting, which is the ecclesial practice of all Christians in preparation for Passover and the resurrection, Athanasius is attentive to the larger theme of fasting and showing kindness to the neighbor. At the same time he addresses the inner personal practice of the soul during fasting. If the inner personal aspect of fasting is not addressed, the larger, corporate fasting of the church will be

30. Cf. 1 Cor 5:7.
31. *Ep. fest.* 14.5.
32. Isa 58:5.
33. *Ep. fest.* 1.4.
34. *Ep. fest.* 1.4.

that of boasting rather than virtue and holiness. For Athanasius, fasting of the soul is required along with the fasting of the body. Virtues and vices are the food of the soul. The soul is nurtured by virtue, righteousness, self-restraint, humbleness, and courage. But if the soul is not nourished by virtue it will feed on sin. The soul should nourish itself on the heavenly bread, not feed on sin.[35] Moses received the law, Elijah received visions, and Daniel received mysteries while fasting. The contemplation of God nourished them instead of food.[36] Food nourishes us externally, but the Word and the contemplation of God is the nourishment of the soul. The Passover lamb, which was a type of the Word, was the divine nourishment of the Jews.[37]

In the *Festal Letters* Athanasius primarily writes about spiritual fasting with little or no emphasis on physical fasting. When he speaks about abstinence he speaks about abstinence from evil for the exercise of virtue.[38] Athanasius advises the following:

> "Let us keep the Feast, not with old leaven, neither with the leaven of malice and wickedness; but with the unleavened bread of sincerity and truth." "Putting off the old man and his deeds, let us put on the new man, which is created in God," in humbleness of mind, and a pure conscience; in meditation of the law by night and by day. And casting away all hypocrisy and fraud, putting far from us all pride and deceit, let us take upon us love towards God and towards our neighbor, that being new [creatures], and receiving the new wine, even the Holy Spirit, we may

---

35. *Ep. fest.* 1.5.
36. *Ep. fest.* 1.6.
37. *Ep. fest.* 1.7.
38. *Ep. fest.* 5.4.

> properly keep the feast, even the month of these new [fruits].[39]

Attentiveness to the mind/*nous*, renewal of creation, one of Athanasius's main theological and spiritual themes, together with the Holy Spirit, are what guide the person as well as the larger Christian body to contemplate God, the aim of the spiritual life. Athanasius dispenses his pastoral advice to his listeners that fasting is a spiritual endeavor: it nourishes the soul and prepares one to contemplate God. It is a personal as well as a communal activity within the church in preparation of Passover.

Athanasius urges his hearers to celebrate Passover with joy and gladness, even though it is about the Lord's death and in spite of the persecutions he and his people are going through.[40] Easter is not for mourning but for joy and gladness because the Lord abolished death with his death and gave humanity life by his death. Christ bade the women following him to his death on the cross not to weep for him because his death was not an event of sorrow but of joy; the one who died for them is alive and the giver of life.[41] We rejoice in Christ's victory over death and we rejoice in our incorruptibility for we were made divine through *theopoiēsis*. Christ's resurrection assures us of our own resurrection, his incorruptibility assures us of our own incorruptibly.[42] In the Festal Letter he sent from his exile in Rome, while he was suffering from Arian persecution, Athanasius exhorted his hearers to celebrate the feast with joy because salvation comes after suffering. For only by suffering for our sake and abolishing death did Christ redeem us. While we are

39. *Ep. fest.* 1.9, citing 1 Cor 5:8 and Eph 4:22–24.
40. *Ep. fest.* 11.13.
41. Luke 23:28.
42. *Ep. fest.* 11.14.

suffering we should not separate ourselves from the love of God but celebrate it in joy, for he nourishes us every day.[43] Athanasius asks his hearers not to be consumed with their present tribulations and the persecutions they are suffering for their faith. These are all temporal. It is more beneficial to think of what is eternal. Present suffering cannot be compared to what awaits in the heavenly kingdom.[44] We just need to know that our suffering is for the truth.[45]

Athanasius takes the opportunity of the yearly crafting of the Festal Letter to address the fear and anxiety of his people. Festal Letter Three was written in 331, before the first exile but during a time of tribulation, which Athanasius describes as follows: "We have been held under restraint by those who afflict us, . . . At all times let us stand firm, but especially now, although many afflictions overtake us, and many heretics are furious against us."[46] It was during a period during which the different Arian factions, especially the Meletians, accused him of many things, including breaking the chalice and murdering bishop Arsenius. He was then summoned to the imperial court to defend himself. His spiritual and pastoral advice to his people is that, though one goes through difficulties, tribulations, and false accusations, it is also a time to give thanks to the Lord. Athanasius begins with giving thanks to God who comforts the afflicted, for Athanasius obeyed the voice of truth that silenced his accusers.[47] His message in the third Festal Letter is that the way to celebrate the feast is through the service of the soul, which is prayer and unceasing thanksgiving. Athanasius uses the parable of the unforgiving servant.

43 *Ep. fest.* 13.6.
44. *Ep. fest.* 13.4.
45. *Ep. fest.* 13.6.
46. *Ep. fest.* 3.1, 5.
47. 2 Cor 7:6.

The Spiritual Life, a Life of Renewal

The one who received the single talent did not use it and was cast out for being unthankful. He neglected grace and hid it from others and was cast out for his wickedness and ingratitude. Athanasius encourages his listeners not to be idle like those who did not use their talents, for this was a sign of unthankfulness. If one is idle and does not cultivate the spirit within, virtue departs and is replaced by unclean spirits, one becomes unfruitful, cares more of the world, and is delivered to its lusts. Unthankful people will quench the spirit within them and thoughts of understanding will depart from them. The purified soul brings forth fruits.[48] The ungrateful and unthankful will end up away from God. Job and David were thankful during their time of tribulations. So now in our time of tribulations we give thanks to the Lord. Though hindered, we will proclaim the word of the Lord; though afflicted, we will sing psalms; and though despised, we will persist in the truth.[49] Athanasius reminds his listeners that only one of the ten lepers was thankful for his healing while the rest were ungrateful. Only one of the lepers returned back and gave glory to God and he was the only one who received more because his faith had made him well.[50] Athanasius tells his listeners that thanksgiving gives believers strength and this feast should be celebrated with thanksgiving.[51] Celebrating Passover is not with meat, fine clothing, and leisure, but rather in glorifying God and offering thanksgiving and praise.[52] The significance of this spiritual message of thanksgiving is that it was delivered at a time of great trials and pain to Athanasius and thus

48. *Ep. fest.* 3.2–4.
49. *Ep. fest.* 3.5.
50. Luke 17:19; *Ep. fest.* 6.3.
51. *Ep. fest.* 3.5.
52. *Ep. fest.* 7.3.

makes the message more powerful because he is setting an example for the whole church.

Athanasius's spiritual practices and advice are based on the Bible and theology. While we discussed representative themes from only a few of his works in this chapter, they can be found throughout his writings. His main spiritual and theological principle is that the incarnation granted humanity a life of renewal, a renewal of God's image within us, through which we are granted incorruptibility and *theopoiēsis*, we become children of God and the dwelling place of the Holy Spirit. Athanasius's understanding of the composition of human person, of a soul endowed with reason/*nous*, plays a great role in his spiritual practice and advice on both the individual and collective levels. Individual spirituality is the building block that shapes collective spirituality. The *nous*/reason guides the individual soul to the contemplation of God and to be in the complete presence of the divine. Individual spirituality guides every person in his/her spiritual and social life. The inner thoughts guide the person in his/her actions, for how can a person be virtuous if the mind is filled with anger or injustice and from the heart proceed evil thoughts? The person with a cleansed heart and mind loves the neighbor, has compassion on the needy, fulfills every action in a spiritual manner, conducts him/herself in righteousness, acts in justice, is in constant prayer, and fulfills everything in a spiritual manner.[53] Individual spirituality fashions individual actions that shape collective spirituality and actions.

QUESTIONS FOR FURTHER DISCUSSION

- What are the theological foundations of Athanasius's spirituality?

53. *Ep. fest.* 19.4–6.

- How did Athanasius's advancement of personal spiritual growth collectively change the larger community and society?
- What are the aspects of pastoral and corporate spirituality for Athanasius?
- How did Athanasius, together with the people of Egypt, endure suffering for their faith and convictions with joy, prayer, and thanksgiving?

SUGGESTIONS FOR FURTHER READING

Contra gentes 19–35
On the Incarnation 1–19; 26–32
Letter to Marcellinus on the Interpretation of the Psalms 1–13;
Festal Letters with special attention to letters 1, 3, 5, 7, 10, 11, 13, 14, and 19.
Life of Antony

Appendix 1

MAP OF ROMAN EMPIRE AROUND THE MEDITERRANEAN WITH CITIES MENTIONED IN THE LIFE OF ATHANASIUS

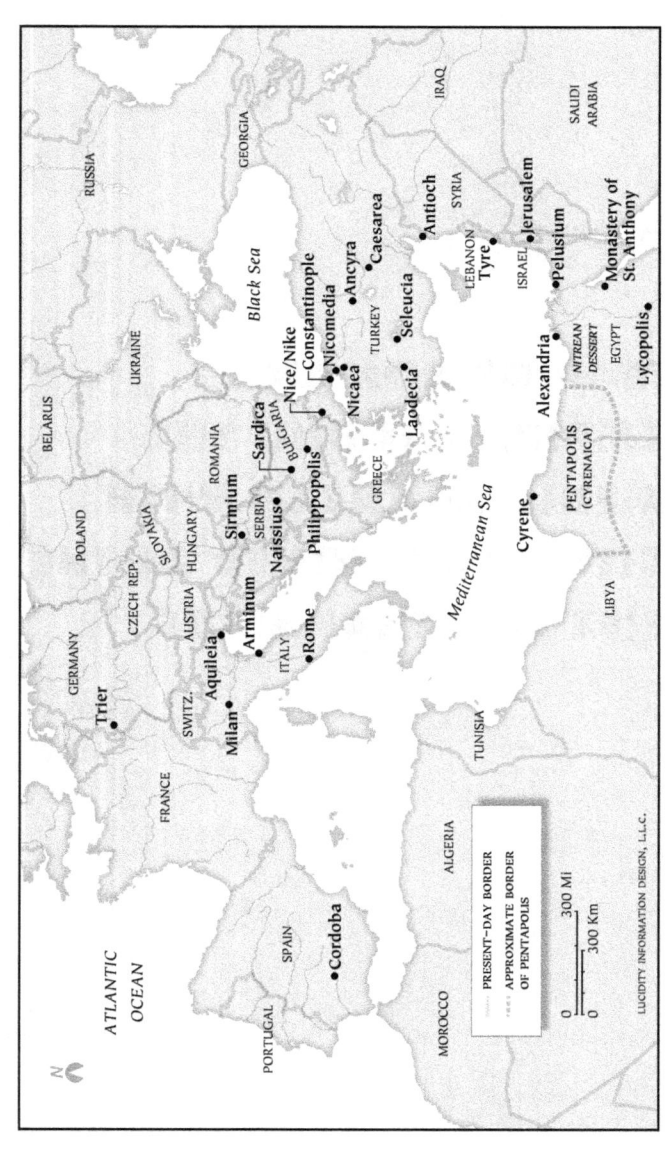

Appendix 2

THE CREED

Nicene Creed AD 325	The Nicaean-Constantinopolitan Creed AD 381
We believe in one God the Father all-powerful, maker of all things both seen and unseen.	We believe in one God the Father all-powerful, maker of heaven and earth, and of all things both seen and unseen.

Appendix 2

And in one Lord Jesus Christ, the Son of God, the only-begotten begotten from the Father; that is from the essence of the Father, God from God, light from light, true God from true God, begotten not made, being of one essence (*homoousion*) with the Father, through whom all things came to be, both those in heaven and those on earth; for us humans and for our salvation he came down and became incarnate, became human, he suffered and rose up on the third day, went up into the heavens, is coming to judge the living and the dead.	And in one Lord Jesus Christ, the only-begotten Son of God, begotten from the Father before all ages, light from light, true God from true God, begotten not made, of one essence with the Father, through whom all things came to be; for us humans and for our salvation he came down from the heavens and became incarnate from the Holy Spirit and the virgin Mary, became human and was crucified on our behalf under Pontius Pilate; he suffered, and was buried and rose up on the third day in accordance with the Scriptures; and went up into heaven and is seated at the Father's right hand; he is coming again with glory to judge the living and the dead; his kingdom will have no end.
And in the Holy Spirit.	And in the Spirit, the holy, the lordly and life-giving one, proceeding forth from the Father, co-worshiped and co-glorified with Father and Son, the one who spoke through the prophets; in one, holy, catholic and apostolic church.

And those who say "there once was when he was not," and "before he was begotten he was not," and that he came to be from things that were not, or from another hypostasis or essence, affirming that the Son of God is subject to change or alteration—these the catholic and apostolic church anathematizes.	
	We confess one baptism for the forgiving of sins. We look forward to a resurrection of the dead and life in the age to come. Amen.

BIBLIOGRAPHY

PRIMARY SOURCES

The Writings of Athanasius of Alexandria

Editions and translations

Athanasius *Athanasius Werke*. Edited by Martin Tetz et al. Multi-volume. Berlin: Walter de Gruyter, 1934–.

———. *Histoire "acéphale" et Index Syriaque des Lettres Festales d'Athanase d'Alexandrie*. Edited by Annik Martin. Sources Chrétiennes 317. Paris: Cerf, 1985.

———. *Later treatises of S. Athanasius, Archbishop of Alexandria: with notes, and an appendix on S. Cyril of Alexandria and Theodoret*. Oxford: Parker, 1881.

———. *The Life of Antony and the Letter to Marcellinus*. Translated by Robert C Gregg. The Classics of Western Spirituality. New York: Paulist, 1980.

———. *The Life of Antony: The Coptic Life and The Greek Life*. Translated by Tim Vivian et al. Cistercian Studies Series 202. Kalamazoo, MI: Cistercian, 2003.

———. *On the Incarnation*, with an introduction by C. S. Lewis. Cambridge: St. Vladimir's Seminary Press, 1993.

Bibliography

———. *Sur L'incarnation Du Verbe*. Edited by Charles Kannengiesser. Sources Chrétiennes 199. Paris: Cerf, 2000.

———. *Vie d'Antoine*. Edited by G. J. M Bartelink. Sources Chrétiennes 400. Paris: Cerf, 1994.

Athanasius and Didymus the Blind. *Works on the Spirit: Athanasius's Letters to Serapion on the Holy Spirit & Didymus's on the Holy Spirit*. Edited and translated by Mark DelCogliano et al. Popular Patristics Series 43. Yonkers, NY: St. Vladimir's Seminary Press, 2011.

Barbard, L. W. *The Monastic Letters of Saint Athanasius the Great*. Oxford: SLG Press, 1994.

Camplani, Alberto. *Le Lettere Festali di Atanasio di Alessandria*. Rome: Centro Italiano Microfiches, 1989.

Casey, R. P. "Armenian Manuscripts of St. Athanasius of Alexandria." *Harvard Theological Review* 24 (1931) 43–59.

Lefort, L. T. *Saint Athanase: Lettres festales et pastorals en Copte*. Scriptores Coptici 19 (1955) 1–72; 20 (1955) 1–55.

Schaff, Philip, and Henry Wace. *Nicene and Post-Nicene Fathers*. Second Series 4. Peabody: Hendrickson, 1995. https://www.ccel.org/fathers.html.

Thomson. Robert W. *Contra gentes and De incarnatione*. Oxford: Clarendon, 1971.

———. "Some Remarks on the Syriac Version of Athanasius' *De Incarnatione*." *Le Museon* 77 (1964) 17–28.

SECONDARY SOURCES

Bibliographical Works

"Athanasius-Bibliographie." http://www.athanasius.theologie.uni-erlangen.de/bibliographie.html.

Dragas, George Dion. *Saint Athanasius of Alexandria: Original Research and New Perspectives*. Patristic Theological Library 1. Rollinsford, NH: Orthodox Research Institute, 2005.

Kannengiesser, C. "The Athanasian decade 1974–84: a bibliographical report." *Theological Studies* 46 (1985) 524–41.

Leemans, J. "Thirteen Years of Athanasius Research (1985–1998): A Survey and Bibliography." *Sacris Erudiri* 39 (2000) 105–217.

Bibliography

Selected Secondary Sources

Anatolios, Khaled. *Athanasius*. The Early Church Fathers. New York: Routledge, 2004.

———. *Retrieving Nicaea: The Development and Meaning of Trinitarian Doctrine*. Grand Rapids: Baker Academic, 2011.

Arnold, Duane W. H. *The Early Episcopal Career of Athanasius of Alexandria*. Notre Dame: University of Notre Dame Press, 1991.

Ayers, Lewis. "Athanasius' Initial Defence of the Term *homoousios*: Rereading the *De Decretis*." *Journal of Early Christian Studies* 12 (2004) 337–59.

Behr, John. *The Nicene Faith*. The Formation of Christian Theology 2, Part 1. Crestwood, NY: St. Vladimir's Seminary Press, 2004.

Brakke, David. *Athanasius and the Politics of Asceticism*. Oxford Early Christian Studies. Oxford: Clarendon, 1995.

———. "The Greek and Syriac versions of the Life of Antony," *Le Muséon* 107 (1994) 29–53.

Donker, Gerald J. *The Text of the Apostolos in Athanasius of Alexandria*. Society of Biblical Literature: The New Testament in the Greek Fathers 8. Atlanta: Society of Biblical Literature, 2011.

Ernest, James D. *The Bible in Athanasius of Alexandria*. The Bible in Ancient Christianity 2. Boston: Brill Academic, 2004.

Farag, Lois. *Balance of the Heart: Desert Spirituality for Twenty-First-Century Christians*. Eugene, OR: Cascade, 2012.

———. "*Organon* in Athanasius' De incarnatione: A Case of Textual Interpolation." In *Studia Patristica Vol. XCV*, edited by Markus Vinzent, 21:93–105. Fourth Century Cappadocian Writers. Leuven: Peeters, 2017.

———. *St. Cyril of Alexandria, a New Testament Exegete: His Commentary on the Gospel of John*. Piscataway, NJ: Gorgias, 2007.

Florovsky, George. "The Concept of Creation in St. Athanasius." *Studia Patristica* 6 (1962) 36–52.

Gwynn, David M. *Athanasius of Alexandria: Bishop, Theologian, Ascetic, Father*. Christian Theology in Context. Oxford: Oxford University Press, 2012.

———. *The Eusebians: The Polemic of Athanasius of Alexandria and the Construction of the "Arian Controversy."* Oxford Theological Monographs. Oxford: Oxford University Press, 2007.

Kannengiesser, Charles. "La date de l'apologie d'Athanase 'Contre les païens' et 'sur l'incarnation.'" *Recherches de Science Religieuse* 58 (1970) 383–428.

Bibliography

Kolp, A. L. "Partakers of the Divine Nature: the Use of 2 Peter 1:4 by Athanasius." *Studia Patristica* 17 (1979) 1018–23.

Kopecek, Thomas A. *A History of Neo-Arianism*. Patristic Monograph Series 8. Cambridge: Philadelphia Patristic Foundation, 1979.

Lienhard, Joseph T. *Contra Marcellum: Marcellus of Ancyra and Fourth-Century Theology*. Washington, DC: Catholic University of America Press, 1999.

Lieu, Samuel N. C. *Manichaeism in the Later Roman Empire and Medieval China*. Rev. and exp. 2nd ed. Wissenschaftliche Untersuchungen Zum Neuen Testament 63. Tübingen: Mohr, 1992.

Meijering, E. P. *Athanasius, Contra Gentes: Introduction, Translation, and Commentary*. Philosophia Patrum 7. Leiden: Brill, 1984.

Norton, Peter. *Episcopal Elections 250–600: Hierarchy and Popular Will in Late Antiquity*. Oxford Classical Monographs. Oxford: Oxford University Press, 2007.

Parvis, Sara. *Marcellus of Ancyra and the Lost Years of the Arian Controversy, 325–345*. Oxford Early Christian Studies. Oxford: Oxford University Press, 2006.

Rubenson, Samuel. *The Letters of St. Antony: Monasticism and the Making of a Saint*. Minneapolis: Fortress, 1995.

Russell, Norman. *The Doctrine of Deification in the Greek Patristic Tradition*. Oxford: Oxford University Press, 2006.

Stead, G. C. "Rhetorical Method in Athanasius." *Vigiliae Christianae* 30 (1985) 121–37.

———. "The *Thalia* of Arius and the Testimony of Athanasius." *Journal of Theological Studies, New Series* 29 (1985) 20–52.

Tovar, Sofia Torallas. "Athanasius' Letter to Dracontius: A Fourth-century Coptic Translation in Papyrus Roll (P.Monts.Roca inv. 14)." *Adamantius* 24 (2018) 43–59.

Vaggione, Richard Paul. *Eunomius of Cyzicus and the Nicene Revolution*. Oxford: Oxford University Press, 2000.

Vivian, Tim. *Saint Peter of Alexandria: Bishop and Martyr*. Studies in Antiquity and Christianity. Philadelphia: Fortress Press, 1988.

Vinzent, Markus. *Asterius von Kappadokien*. Leiden: Brill, 1993.

Williams, Rowan. *Arius: Heresy and Tradition*. 2nd ed. London: SCM, 2001.

Worp, K. A. "A Checklist of Bishops in Byzantine Egypt (A.D. 325-c. 750)." *Zeitschrift fur Papyrologie und Epigraphik* 100 (1994) 283–318.

Young, Frances M. *The Making of the Creeds*. SCM Classics. London: SCM Press, 2002.

SUBJECT INDEX

activity, See *energeia*
Aetius, 20, 73, 80
Against the Pagans, ix, 77,
    123, 137, 141, 153
    C. Gent., ix, 28–37, 138–39
    Contra gentes, ix, 28–29,
    41–42, 52, 153
Alexander of Alexandria,
    Pope, x, 3–6, 78–79, 81
allegorizing, ≤8
Antony of Egypt/the Great, x,
    xii, 19, 20, 25–27, 47–52,
    60, 137, 141–42, 145,
    153, 161, 163–64
Apol. Const., See *Defense
    before Constantius*
Apologia ad Constantium,
    See *Defense before
    Constantius*
Apologia de fuga sua, See
    Defense of His Flight
Apol. Sec., See *Defense against
    the Arians*

*Apologia secunda Apologia
    contra Arianos*, See *Defense against the Arians*
Aquileia, 13, 156
Aristotle, x, 34, 112–13, 118,
    Aristotle, *Metaphysics*,
    34
Arius, x, 4–5, 8, 13, 19,
    57–58, 62, 67, 78–79, 92
Asterius the Sophist, 13,
    78–80, 88, 164

Basil of Ancyra, 20–21
Basil of Caesarea, 22, 28
Basilides, 78, 82–83
begotten, 20, 38, 60, 79, 91,
    95–98, 158–59
    only-begotten, 38, 80–81,
    158
    unbegotten, 20, 79–81, 84

C. Ar., See *Orations against
    the Arians*

Subject Index

C. Gent., See Against the Pagans
Circular Letter, ix
  Ep. encycl., ix, 10–11
  Epistula encyclica, ix
Communicatio idiomatum, 64, 95
Constans, emperor (337–50), 9, 15–17
Constantine, emperor (r. 306–37), 2, 4, 7–9, 12
Constantinus, emperor (337–40), 9
Constantius, emperor (337–61), 9–12, 14–22,
contemplate, 30, 32–35, 38, 49, 92, 99, 138–40, 149
Contra gentes, See Against the Pagans
corruptible, 41, 45, 90, 103
  incorruptible, 41, 45–46, 103, 127–28, 132, 140
  incorruption, 42, 44–45, 72–73, 124–25, 130, 132–33
  incorruptibility, 44, 46, 108, 123, 128, 149, 152
Council
  of Ariminum, x, 19, 20, 21, 110
  of Dedication, 14
  of Milan, 16
  of Nicaea, 3–5, 6, 8, 12, 14, 16, 58–59, 64, 74, 81
  of Sardica, 11, 15–16
  of Seleucia, 19–21
create/created, 4, 20, 27–29, 32, 34–35, 37, 39–40, 43, 45–46, 50, 55, 57–58, 61, 63–64, 66–70, 75, 79–80, 82, 85–89, 92, 94–95, 97–98, 104–5, 114, 119, 123, 125–28, 137–39, 145–46, 148
created being/entity/humanity, 4. 28, 34, 38, 40, 55, 57–58, 64, 68, 72, 75, 80, 84–86, 89, 91–93, 98–99, 104, 108, 114, 116–19, 126–27, 133, 137
  recreate, 41, 140
  uncreated, 72, 87, 123
creation, vii, 25, 28–29, 34–39, 41–42, 44–46, 49, 51–52, 57, 63–64, 72, 79–82, 85–87, 92, 95–97, 106, 114, 116, 119–20, 138–39, 141, 149, 163
Creed, 5, 14–15, 17, 19–21, 99
  Anomean, 21
  "Dated," 20–21
  Dedication, 21
  Lucianic, 21
  Nicene or of Nicaea, 5, 15, 17, 21–22, 81, 99, 104, 108–9, 157–59
  of Acacius, 21
  of Constantinople, 109, 157
  of Nice, 21
  of Theophronius, 21
  Sirmium (1 & 2), 21

De incarnatione, See *On The Incarnation*
De decretis, See, *Defense of the Nicene Definition*
De sententia Dionysii, See *On the Opinion of Dionysius*
De synodis, See *On the Councils of Ariminum and Seleucia*

Subject Index

Decr., See Defense of the Nicene Definition
Defense against the Arians, ix, 24
  Apol. Sec., ix, 8, 10
  Apologia secunda Apologia contra Arianos, ix, 8
Defense before Constantius, ix, 18–19
  Apol. Const., ix
  Apologia ad Constantium, ix, 18
Defense of His Flight, x, 18–19
  Fug., x
  Apologia de fuga sua, x, 8, 18
Defense of the Nicene Definition, ix, 16, 24
  Decr., ix, 79–80, 130
  De decretis, ix, 16–17, 24, 163
Dion., See On the Opinion of Dionysius
Dionysius of Alexandria, Pope, ix, 17
Dionysius, Church of, 23
double accounts, 61–64, 75, 95
Dracontius, 17, 164

Edessa, 22
Edict of Milan, 2
Encyclical Letter of Alexander concerning the Deposition of Arius, x, 14
  Hen. Som., x, 14
  Henos somatos, x
energeia, xiv, xv, 86, 88, 111–23, 133–35
  activity, xiv, 81, 86–87, 90, 95, 102–3, 111–12, 114–16, 119, 121–22, 133–35
Ep. Adelph., See Letter to Adelphius
Ep. Aeg. Lib., See Letter to the Bishops of Egypt and Libya
Ep. Afr. See Letter to the Bishops of Africa
Ep. encycl. See Circular Letter
Ep. Epict., See Letter to Epictetus
Ep. fest., See Festal Letters
Ep. Marcell., See Letter to Marcellinus on the Interpretation of the Psalms
Ep. Max., See Letter to Maximus
Ep. mon.1&2, See First or Second Letter to the Monks
Ep. Serap., See Letters to Serapion concerning the Holy Spirit
Epistula Ad Adelphium, See Letter to Adelphius
Epistula ad Afros episcopos, See Letter to the Bishops of Africa
Epistula ad Epictetum, See Letter to Epictetus
Epistula ad episcopos Aegypti et Libyae, See Letter to the Bishops of Egypt and Libya
Epistula ad Marcellinum de interpretatione Psalmorum, See Letter to Marcellinus on the Interpretation of the Psalms

Subject Index

Epistula ad Maximum, See *Letter to Maximus*
Epistula ad monachos, See *First* or *Second Letter to the Monks*
Epistula ad Serapionem, See *Letters to Serapion concerning the Holy Spirit*
Epistula encyclica, See *Circular Letter*
Epistula festales, See *Festal Letters*
Eunomius, 20, 78, 80
Eusebians, 2, 4, 8–10, 78–79
Eusebius, *Historia ecclesiastica*, the same for Socrates and Sozomen *Historia ecclesiastica*, Hist. eccl., x, 2–3
Eusebius of Nicomedia, 7, 9, 13, 78–79
evil, 26–29, 31, 34–35, 40, 45, 50–52, 56, 71, 81, 111, 139, 140, 147–48, 152
exile, xiii, 1, 5, 7–10, 13–14, 16, 18–23, 146, 149, 150

Festal Letters, x, 6, 18, 24, 68, 136–37, 142, 146, 148, 153
  Ep. fest., x, 68, 73–74, 137, 143
  Epistula festales, x
First or *Second Letter to the Monks*, x
  Ep. mon.1&2,x, 84
  Epistula ad monachos, x
Fug., See *Defense of His Flight*

George of Cappadocia (356–61), 11–12, 16, 18–19

Gregory Nazianzus (329–90), vi, 3, 11, 22, 112, 123, 134
Gregory of Cappadocia (339–45), 10–13, 15

H. Ar. See *History of the Arians*
Hen. Som., See *Encyclical Letter of Alexander concerning the Deposition of Arius*
Henos sonatos, See *Encyclical Letter of Alexander concerning the Deposition of Arius*
Hist. eccl., See Eusebius, *Historia ecclesiastica*
*Hist.*x, 3, See Rufinus, *Eusebii Historia ecclessiastica*
Historia Arianorum, See *History of the Arians*
History of the Arians, x, 11, 16–17, 19, 24
  H. Ar., x, 11–12
  Historia Arianorum, x, 16, 19, 24
Holy Spirit, xiv, 20, 22, 53, 65–66, 70, 72, 75, 77–78, 81–82, 84–88, 91–92, 104–11, 113–18, 123, 133, 135, 148–49, 152, 158
Hosius of Cordoba, 9, 15–16

immortal/immortality, 26, 29–33, 39, 40–41, 44–45, 51, 72–73, 91, 103, 108, 130, 132–33, 137–41
Inc. See *On The Incarnation*
incarnation/incarnate, xiv, 26–27, 35, 38–46,

Subject Index

50–51, 55, 58, 62, 64–65,
67–72, 77–79, 84–85,
90, 94, 95–97, 100–102,
107–8, 112, 116, 118–20,
122–30, 132–36, 140–41,
145, 148
incorruption/incorruptible/
incorruptibility, *See*
corruptible
interpretation, double accounts, 61–64, 75, 95
shadow, 68, 70–71, 73–74
spiritual, 54, 71–76
theological, 56, 61, 68–71,
75–76
type, 68, 70–71, 73–74, 148
typology, 73

John of Acraph, 7
Jovian, emperor, 22–24
Julian, emperor, 22
Julius of Rome, 9, 13–15

Letter to Adelphius, ix, 23, 135
  Ep. Adelph., ix, 59, 70, 83,
  119–21, 131
  Epistula Ad Adelphium, ix
Letter to Epictetus, ix, 23, 110
  Ep. Epict., ix, 42, 101–2
  Epistula ad Epictetum, ix
Letter to Marcellinus on the
  Interpretation of the
  Psalms, x, 143–44, 153
  Ep. Marcell., x, 144–45
  *Epistula ad Marcellinum de
  interpretatione Psalmorum*, x
Letter to Maximus, x
  Ep. Max., 133
  Epistula ad Maximum, x
*Letters to Serapion concerning
  the Holy Spirit*, x, 19,
  21–22, 77, 82, 105–6,
  108, 110, 135
  Ep. Serap., x, 65, 78, 86–87,
  105–6, 113–16, 130
  Epistula ad Serapionem, x
Letter to the Bishops of Africa,
  ix
  Ep. Afr., ix, 5, 59, 89, 127
  Epistula ad Afros episcopos,
  ix
*Letter to the Bishops of Egypt
  and Libya*, ix, 8, 19, 54
  Ep. Aeg. Lib., ix, 59, 70, 83,
  119–21, 131
  Epistula ad episcopos Aegypti et Libyae, ix, 8
Liberius of Rome, 9, 16
Life of Antony, x, xii, 19,
  25–27, 47–52, 60, 137,
  141, 144–45, 153
  Vit. Ant., x, 47, 49–50
  Vita Antonii, x, 20
Logos, xiii, 32, 36, 39, 42–45,
  51, 91, 138
logoi, 36
LXX, *See* Septuagint

Magnentius, 17–18
Marcellus of Ancyra, 13, 15
martyrdom, 23, 26, 39,
  44–45, 48
Melitians, 6–8, 19, 81, 83
Melitius of Lycopolis, 6,
  81–82
Metaph./Metaphysics See
  Aristotle
Milan, 13, 156
mind, 27, 30–34, 39, 43,
  46–47, 71–73, 84,
  138–39, 142–43, 145,
  148, 149, 152
  See also *nous*

Subject Index

monastic/s, 10, 25–26, 48–50
monasticism, 20, 47
monoenergeia/ oneness of energy, 71
monoenergism, 122
movement, 29–32, 34, 138, 144
unmovable mover, 34

Nicaea, 59, 74, 156
Nicaean faith, 15, 23, 74,
See Creed, Nicene or of Nicaea
Naissius, 13, 156
Nice, 21, 156
Nous, 31–32, 34–36, 38, 43, 45–46, 48–51, 138–39, 141, 143, 145, 149, 152
See also mind, reason

On the Councils of Ariminum and Seleucia, x, 19, 24, 110
Syn., x, 4, 14, 58, 79, 80, 104, 130
De synodis, x, 19, 20, 21, 24
On the Opinion of Dionysius, ix
De sententia Dionysii, ix, 17
Dion., ix
Origen of Alexandria, 17, 33, 57
On The Incarnation, x, xii, 7, 25–27, 38, 45–46, 50, 52, 60, 77, 123, 137, 141, 153
Inc., x, 27–29, 30, 33, 39–40, 43, 45–46, 108, 112, 123–24, 132, 139, 140
De incarnatione, x, 28–29, 41–42

only-begotten, *See* begotten
Orations against the Arians, ix, 13, 17, 59, 76–77, 109, 135
C. Ar., ix, 4, 37, 42, 45, 55–56, 58–60, 62–69, 72, 78–80, 82–83. 85–94, 96, 103, 106–8, 117–19, 121, 124–29, 131–32, 145
Orationes contra Arianos, ix, 37
Orationes contra Arianos,
See Orations against the Arians
originate, 90–91, 96, 127

pastoral, 17, 68, 136–37, 145–53.
persecution, 2, 5–6, 9, 15–16, 24, 80, 144, 146, 149–50
Peter of Alexandria, Pope, 2–3, 6, 81
Philippopolis, 15, 156
Plato, 29, 31
Platonic, 26–27, 31
prayer, 48–49, 141, 143–47, 150, 152–53
Princ., x, 33
Psalms, 49, 59, 106, 143–45, 151

rational, 31–33, 37, 40–41, 50, 138, 142
rationality, 30, 33, 43
rationale, 45
reason, 26, 30–32, 34, 36, 38–39, 43, 45–46, 91, 124, 138, 152
recreate, *See* create
renew/renewal, xiii, 25–27, 30, 39, 41–44, 46–51, 58, 64, 67, 69, 86,-7, 90,

Subject Index

94, 98, 101, 106, 114, 123–25, 127, 133, 136, 138–42, 145, 149, 152
Republic, Plato, x, 29, 31
rhetoric, 3, 36
Rome, 10, 13, 146, 149, 156
Rufinus, *Eusebii Historia ecclessiastica a Rufino translate et continuata Hist.*, x, 3

salvation, xiii, xiv, 4, 23, 26, 40, 51, 68, 70–71, 73, 98, 100–102, 111–12, 132, 134, 137, 139–41, 145, 149, 158
Sardica, 13, 15, 158
Seleucia, 19, 20, 21, 156
senses, 31–34, 38, 49, 51, 55–56, 123, 138–41
Septuagint/LXX, 57, 61, 63–64, 72, 95, 101, 105
sin, *See* transgression
Skopos, 58–59, 69, 74
soul, 26–27, 29–35, 37–39, 43, 46–52. 101, 124, 138–45, 147–52
spirituality, xiii, xiv, xv, 20, 25–26, 32, 46, 48–51, 53–54, 136–53
  See also interpretation, spiritual
Stoic, 36
Syn., See On the Councils of Ariminum and Seleucia

Thalia, 4, 13, 19, 79
Theonas, Church of, 18
Theophronius of Tyana, 14

Theopoiēsis, xiv, xv, 41, 67, 111–12, 123–35, 136, 140, 149, 152
Theopoiēthōmen, xv, 46, 112, 123–24, 132, 135, 140
Tom., See Tome to the People of Antioch
Tome to the People of Antioch, x, 110
  Tom., x, 101
  Tomus ad Antiochenos, x, 108
Tomus ad Antiochenos, See Tome to the People of Antioch
transgression, 27, 40–41, 51, 103, 127, 139
  sin, 40, 64, 96, 102–3, 148, 159
Trier, 8–9, 13, 156
Tropikoi, 22, 78, 82, 105, 113–14
typology, see interpretation, type

unbegotten, *See* begotten
uncreated, *See* create
unoriginate, 20, 84, 88, 90–91, 96, 117

Valens, emperor, 23
Vit. Ant., See Life of Antony
Vita Antonii, See Life of Antony

wisdom, 40, 57–58, 61–62, 66, 79–80, 83–85, 88–90, 93, 108

www.ingramcontent.com/pod-product-compliance
Lightning Source LLC
Chambersburg PA
CBHW020850160426
43192CB00007B/866